TABLE OF CONT

Top 20 Test Taking Tips

1. Carefully follow all the test registration procedures
2. Know the test directions, duration, topics, question types, how many questions
3. Setup a flexible study schedule at least 3-4 weeks before test day
4. Study during the time of day you are most alert, relaxed, and stress free
5. Maximize your learning style; visual learner use visual study aids, auditory learner use auditory study aids
6. Focus on your weakest knowledge base
7. Find a study partner to review with and help clarify questions
8. Practice, practice, practice
9. Get a good night's sleep; don't try to cram the night before the test
10. Eat a well balanced meal
11. Know the exact physical location of the testing site; drive the route to the site prior to test day
12. Bring a set of ear plugs; the testing center could be noisy
13. Wear comfortable, loose fitting, layered clothing to the testing center; prepare for it to be either cold or hot during the test
14. Bring at least 2 current forms of ID to the testing center
15. Arrive to the test early; be prepared to wait and be patient
16. Eliminate the obviously wrong answer choices, then guess the first remaining choice
17. Pace yourself; don't rush, but keep working and move on if you get stuck
18. Maintain a positive attitude even if the test is going poorly
19. Keep your first answer unless you are positive it is wrong
20. Check your work, don't make a careless mistake

Bilingual Education

Foundations of Bilingual Education

Language Proficiency Assessment Committee

<u>Duties and time requirements of the LPAC</u>
The Language Proficiency Assessment Committee (LPAC) fulfills its responsibilities throughout the school year in a cycle. Students with limited English-language proficiency (LEP), students who are considered to speak English as a second language (ESL), or students who are considered English language learners (ELLs) complete forms including a Home Language Survey. The Committee's time requirements begin when a student who identifies a language other than English on the Home Language Survey enrolls in school. The LPAC is required to review documented evidence of student language proficiency and academic status and recommend student placement in an ESL, mainstream, or bilingual educational program within 20 school days/four weeks of student enrollment. The Committee also is required to obtain the parents' permission within this time period. LPAC responsibilities include recommending appropriate interventional and instructional methods; identifying state options for criterion-referenced assessments; helping eligible LEP students participate in other special programs; assuring parental notice of the Committee's decisions for the student and of student progress; and ongoing monitoring of interventions, test results, and program suitability.

<u>Forms used by the Texas Education Agency LPAC relative to LEP/ESL/ELL students, their parents, and the associated educational programs</u>
LPAC issues a Home Language Survey to determine students' first languages and an Initial Review form for Bilingual/ESL education programs. The Parental Notification Form of the Identification and Placement of students in these programs is available in both English and Spanish. LPAC provides one form outlining benefits of Bilingual Education Programs and another form describing benefits of ESL education programs. LPAC supplies a form for the LEP (Limited English Proficiency) Student titled "Plan to Accelerate English Language Proficiency." LPAC provides another form titled "Annual End of Year Review" for Bilingual/ESL educational programs. It publishes a form for monitoring students who have exited Bilingual/ESL programs. The LPAC furnishes a form to the parents of Bilingual/ESL students titled, "Parental Report on Student Progress," also published in Spanish. LPAC activities meet requirements in Title III of the No Child Left Behind Act (NCLB, 2001); and 19 TAC Chapter 19, Subchapter BB of the Commissioner's Rules Concerning State Plan for Educating Limited English Proficient Students, for Texas.

Basic areas of responsibility

The responsibilities of the Texas LPAC include identifying students as English Language Learners (ELLs), having English as a second language (ESL), and/or having limited English proficiency (LEP); the assessment of such students; the review of documents indicating their English language proficiency; their placement in appropriate instructional programs; the identification and selection of appropriate educational interventions and teaching methods for such students; collaboration by the involved parties; annual reviews of students' progress in the programs selected for them; assessment of student performance and progress; and notification of the students' parents. The LPAC's identification and placement includes criteria for identifying students as LEP; reviewing legally mandated assessment instruments; and the placement process. Interventions and instructional methods include techniques and strategies for teaching Beginning English (BE) and ESL, and a student plan for accelerating English-language proficiency. Annual reviews include spring and end-of-year LPAC meetings reviewing student progress and recommending future placement. Students are also monitored after program exit.

State of Texas Assessments of Academic Readiness (STAAR) program

STAAR replacment of TAKS

Whereas the State of Texas Assessments of Academic Readiness (STAAR) program replaced the Texas Assessment of Knowledge and Skills (TAKS) program for grades 3-8 in the 2011-2012 school year, this change was intended to be phased in for the high school grade levels. Students initially enrolling in ninth grade take the STAAR. Those students repeating the ninth grade are given the TAKS to qualify for graduation. The STAAR Alternate replaces the TAKS Alternate only for those ELL students also receiving special education services who are eligible for alternate assessment based upon alternative achievement standards and content. Other than this exception, the TAKS system will stay in place only for grades 10 and higher. ELL students who do not meet the participation requirements for other TAKS assessments will take the TAKS Grade 10 assessment. Those students ineligible for other TAKS assessments and also ineligible for limited English proficiency (LEP) postponements at exit level will take the TAKS Exit Level assessment.

Requirements for English Language Learners (ELLs)

All ELL students must take STAAR assessments in grades 3-8 and end-of-course (EOC) assessments, with no exemptions allowed. In the 2011-2012 school year, STAAR replaced the Texas Assessment of Knowledge and Skills (TAKS) for grades 3-9. ELLs and non-ELLs in bilingual/dual-language programs for whom Spanish assessment best measures school progress take the STAAR Spanish 3-5. ELLs for whom Spanish is not the best measure or for whom no Spanish-language version exists, ELL students who have not achieved advanced high ratings on Texas English Language Proficiency Assessment System (TELPAS) reading, ELL students who have been enrolled in U.S. schools for three or fewer school years, and ELL students who qualify as unschooled ELL refugees/asylees enrolled in U.S. schools for five or fewer school years all take STAAR L 3-8 and STAAR L EOC for Math, Science, and Social Studies subject areas only. STAAR Modified and Alternate 3-8 and EOC are for ELLs receiving special education services and meeting specific participation requirements based on their special education needs. ELLS not meeting these requirements take STAAR's 3-8 and EOC Primary State Assessments.

Subjects assessed - elementary and middle grades vs. high school
The State of Texas Assessments of Academic Readiness (STAAR) replaces the Texas Assessment of Knowledge and Skills (TAKS) as of Spring 2012 in elementary and middle school (3-8) grades. Both the TAKS and STAAR assessments test students' attainment of the Texas Essential Knowledge and Skills (TEKS) curriculum standards. The STAAR tests for grades 3-8 assess the same subjects as did the TAKS tests. However, in high school, the former tests specified for each grade from 9 to 12 will be replaced by end-of-course (EOC) assessments in the subjects of English I, II, and III; world history; U.S. history; world geography; biology; chemistry; geometry; physics; and Algebra I and II. Specific STAAR tests for English Language Learner (ELL) students include the STAAR L and STAAR Spanish. Specific STAAR tests for special education students include the STAAR Alternate and the STAAR Modified.

Modification guidelines for STAAR-M provided by the TEA

Assessments in all test subjects for ELLs for grades 3-8
When administering STAAR-M assessments to ELLs in all grade 3-8 subjects, teachers should decrease the number of questions tested. Font sizes of text and graphics should be enlarged. Educators should clarify information given for questions, add background information, revise given information, and/or add context for the question. Vocabulary not specific to the subject and complex sentence structures should be simplified. Teachers can delete one answer choice in multiple-choice questions. They can delete questions they cannot modify based on guidelines given by the TEA. Where applicable, teachers also can delete exception questions (asking "except" or "not"). They can delete the additional parts of compound answer choices. Direct questions can be changed to open-ended statements, and vice versa. Questions in passive voice can be converted to active voice. Superfluous information in the questions and/or illustrations can be removed. Where it applies, teachers can draw students' attention to included graphics. They also can enlarge the white spaces around and inside of test graphics used, such as charts, tables, maps, etc.

Assessments in math and science subjects for grades 3-8 ELL students
For grade 3-8 STAAR math tests, teachers should supply practice grids and directions for gridable questions; for grade 6-8 levels they should use modified grids. For math tests, should point out the ruler in state-supplied reference materials, and they should point out the periodic table of elements in materials for science tests. For science tests only, teachers may delete gridable questions entirely. Also only on science tests, when a defined, subject-specific term that is not tested appears in a question, they should place it in a text box in boldface, or place its

- 7 -

definition in parenthesis following the term. On both the math and science tests, teachers should break complex questions into smaller meaningful pieces using bullets. When suitable, they should simplify numbers and decrease variables in questions. In multiple-step questions, they can decrease the number of steps/operations. Where applicable, they should insert text boxes giving needed formulas/conversions into questions. To explain processes such measuring, they should supply specific instructions.

Assessments in social studies for grades 3-8 ELL students

When teachers are administering the STAAR-M (State of Texas Assessments of Academic Readiness-Modified) assessments in social studies to English Language Learner (ELL) students in grades 3-8, they can make some modifications to facilitate ELLs' ability to understand and respond best to the test items. Guidelines from the Texas Education Agency (TEA) focus on the language found in many historical documents. For example, when excerpts are quoted from older documents (for example, the U.S. Declaration of Independence and the U.S. Constitution) and the language is archaic, ELL students will not be as able to adjust to the language usage as can native English-speaking students. This inability is also true for complex language. Teachers can replace unfamiliar or difficult language with simplified English marked by brackets. They can add text explaining this language, also in brackets. When historical excerpts or quotations are lengthy, teachers can shorten them, marking the deletion of parts by using ellipses (....).

Assessments in Reading for grades 3-8 ELL students

Teachers can help ELL students in grades 3-8 perform to their best abilities on the STAAR-M (State of Texas Assessments of Academic Readiness-Modified) Reading assessment by giving them pre-reading text. Such pre-reading text identifies the topic, introduces unfamiliar and difficult vocabulary words and names (including pronunciation keys as needed), explains hard concepts, and gives a general purpose for reading a given selection. Teachers should read this pre-reading text to ELL students before the students read the provided selection independently. Prose reading and editing selections can be separated into smaller sections, with the associated questions placed immediately following each section. For grades 4-8, STAAR selections paired can be given separately. Teachers also can edit STAAR questions by replacing non-tested figurative language with more literal language. Wherever it will not make the sentence structure awkward, the teacher also can remove or restrict the use of contractions in reading selections.

Assessments in reading and writing for grades 3-8 ELL students in tested writing tasks

When teachers administer the STAAR-M in Reading and Writing for grades 3-8 to ELL students, they may have divided selections provided in the test into smaller, more manageable sections or "chunks," with only the questions pertinent to each chunk following it. They then can modify editing questions that test student writing by removing all the distractors (wrong answers) for a given question from the corresponding chunk. For writing revision questions, teachers can provide ELL

- 8 -

students with scaffolding (support) for text content by dividing questions with multiple sentences into single sentences and making them visually simpler by placing spaces between sentences. Teachers should use simpler, more direct language in all prompts for writing tasks in the test. Another way to assist ELL students in their writing performance on the STAAR-M involves adjusting teacher expectations regarding student vocabulary range and spelling by scoring these students' compositions based on a modified three-point rubric.

Teachers should have modified some reading selections provided in the STAAR-M Reading assessment for grades 3-8 to accommodate their ELL students. Accordingly, teachers will then need to make matching modifications in the test questions based on those selections. For example, they may delete some questions about material they have removed from the selections and/or edit other questions corresponding to deleted selection parts. Where teachers have divided selections into smaller segments and placed the relevant questions after each segment, question distractors should come from that segment or the one before it if needed. Teachers should supply definitions of literary terms as needed. They also may forgo testing ELL students in grades 4-8 on the ability to connect across different texts by removing all thematically related questions that cross over paired selections and only test vocabulary in this reporting category (Reporting Category 1 on the STAAR-M, Reading).

Participation requirements TAKS-M and the TAKS Accommodated

ELLs meeting TAKS exemption criteria due to Limited English Proficiency (LEP) or otherwise eligible for Linguistically Accommodated Testing (LAT) as "unschooled" refugees or asylees are given TAKS' LAT for Grade 10 Math, Science, and English Language Arts subjects. TAKS-M and/or LAT eligibility for ELLs receiving special education services are based on their special education needs, not on their second language acquisition needs. Such students meeting specific requirements identified by the Texas Education Agency (TEA) take the TAKS-M for grades 10 and 11. Such students whose Admissions, Review, and Dismissal (ARD) Committees determine their special education needs are met by taking regular TAKS tests with specific accommodations take TAKS (Accommodated) Grade 10 and Exit Level tests. Those meeting both TAKS-M and LAT participation requirements take the TAKS-M LAT for Grade 10; Exit Level; and Math, English Language Arts, and Science, which incorporate the TAKS (Accommodated)'s format accommodations.

Requirements participating in the TELPAS tests

Only ELL (English Language Learner) students are given the TELPAS tests. TELPAS assessments for grades K-12 measure Listening, Reading, Speaking, and Writing. K-12 students take these tests until they are classified as non-LEP (non-Limited English Proficiency) by meeting the tests' exit criteria. A recently introduced requirement mandates that grade 2-12 ELL students not speaking English and starting school in the school year's second semester no longer automatically receive a Beginning rating without first taking the Reading test. Instead, scores based on student achievement on the Reading test are used. Assessment decisions for students dually receiving ELL and special education services are made jointly by the Language Proficiency Assessment Committee (LPAC) and the Admission, Review and Dismissal (ARD) Committee, who collaborate to consider both a student's second-language acquisition needs and special education needs. Occasionally, due to specific disabilities, LPAC and ARD may decide not to assess some students in certain domains. At testing time, these students are reported using the score code "ARD Decision."

Raw scores vs. scale scores on the TELPAS

TELPAS raw scores can be interpreted only for specific test questions. Scale scores can be interpreted across various questions and test administrations. Scale scores convert raw scores onto scales that all assessments' test forms share in common. The scale score accounts for the difficulty level of the particular test question. Individual student test results can be compared against proficiency levels or passing standards. For example, on the Reading test for Grade 2 (Spring 2011), a Raw Score of 0 = Scale Score of 262; Raw Score 18 = Scale Score 545. Scale scores up to 550 equate to Beginning proficiency levels. 19 Raw Score = 551 Scale Score; Raw Score 29 = 609 Scale Score; Scale Scores 551-614 = Intermediate proficiency levels. Raw Score 30 = Scale Score 615; Raw Score 38 = Scale Score 663; Scale Scores 615-669 = Advanced proficiency levels. Raw Score 39 = Scale Score 670; Raw Score 49 = Scale Score 850; Scale Scores 67+ equal Advanced High proficiency levels.

Bilingual Education Act and its influence on ensuing related court cases

Bilingual education in America has existed since the 17th century, when Polish immigrants with needed industries and skills in the Virginia colony were granted the "rights of Englishmen" and established the first bilingual schools. In the 18th century, Catholic missionaries used Native American languages to teach Christianity to American Indians. In the 19th century, many bilingual schools had developed to address immigration, with Ohio the first state to pass a law for bilingual education. However, during World War I, nativists afraid of foreign influences eradicated most bilingual programs. Interest in bilingual education returned with the 20th-century Civil Rights Movement, motivated by interests in educational desegregation, placement for children with disabilities, and instruction in native languages. The 1968 Bilingual Education Act, Title VII of the Elementary and Secondary Education Act (ESEA), triggered a number of court cases promoting native-language testing, testing without racial discrimination, affirmative measures by schools to remedy student language deficiencies, and acknowledgement of English-language dialects like African-American/Black English.

Significant U.S. Supreme Court decisions related to bilingual education

In the case of Diana vs. State Board of Education (1971), the U.S. Supreme Court ruled that schools testing students to determine eligibility for special education services must administer such tests in the students' native languages. In Larry P. vs. Riles (1972), the Court determined that schools are responsible to provide tests that do not discriminate based on race. Lack of English-language proficiency prevented students from understanding academic subjects taught only in English when a large class of Chinese parents filed suit on their children's behalf. Consequently, in Lau vs. Nichols (1974), the Court ruled school districts must take "affirmative steps" to correct students' linguistic deficiencies. In Martin Luther King, Jr. Elementary Children vs. Ann Arbor School District Board of Education (1979), the Court ordered that teachers in Ann Arbor, Michigan receive linguistic instruction in Black English as a legitimate American English dialect. In Castañeda vs. Pickard (1981), the Court ruled school districts must make "appropriate action to overcome language barriers" and established standards for evaluating districts' action(s).

Recent reactions in the U.S. both for and against bilingual education programs

In the United States, many proponents of bilingual education programs argue that school instruction that addresses the needs of LEP, ESL, and ELL students is the most reasonable approach, since these students obviously cannot learn academic subjects taught only in English with the same levels of success as English-speaking students. Proponents also point out that the bilingual educational approach is also a democratic one befitting a democratic political system and society. Many of those who oppose bilingual education claim that the American educational system, historically and currently, enables upward mobility for all citizens who are "willing to work." Furthermore, some opponents of bilingual instruction also argue that providing only a monolingual (English) and monocultural American education is necessary to preserving the American identity: these opponents fear that allowing multiple linguistic and cultural influences would destroy our nation. Others supporting bilingualism maintain that educational pluralism is not so much a remedial exercise as a belated confirmation of the existing social reality.

Contemporary issues in California

One recent educational issue that developed in Oakland, California, concerned a controversy over "Ebonics," i.e. African-American English dialect. As this dialect became more prevalent, public school educators in Oakland responded by making a positive effort to use this social reality to further student achievement. They acknowledged that some of their students spoke in Ebonics. They did not support teaching in Ebonics, but they did use the dialect overtly to provide a starting point for helping those students to learn and perform better, and to make the transition to using standard English effectively in academic and social contexts. While this trend has since undergone modifications, it has not been completely abandoned. Another issue that emerged in the state of California was Proposition 227 (1998). This law requires California schools to teach LEP/ELL students in "structured immersion" classes almost completely in English for one year and then transition them to mainstream classes. This is significant in the state of California, since this state has more ELL students than any other state—at least one out of three.

California bilingual education

<u>Two 1998 California legislative events</u>
California's Board of Education had been sued in 1997 by plaintiffs claiming that Limited English Proficient (LEP) students' rights were violated by the Board's granting waivers to school districts allowing English immersion to replace bilingual education. The judge's 1998 ruling was (1) that the State Board of Education did not have the authority to grant such waivers, but also (2) that California state law did not apply to bilingual education and only Federal laws applied. The first part of this ruling restricted state departure from bilingual education programs; however, the second part conversely restricted enforcement of state laws to provide bilingual education. Also in 1998, California's governor vetoed State Senate Bill 6. On one hand, SB6 incorporated many provisions of the 1974 Chacón-Moscone Bilingual-Bicultural Education Act, which had initiated transitional bilingual education programs meeting Federal guidelines for identifying, placing, and re-classifying LEP students. On the other hand, SB6 also allowed local school districts flexibility in choosing bilingual or English-immersion programs. As a result, its veto both impeded and protected bilingual education.

<u>Outcomes of legislation in 1996-1998</u>
California's bilingual education laws affect the entire USA, both because certain state laws must comply with Federal laws and because, with the nation's highest percentage of linguistic minorities in California, its laws influence the rest of the country. In 1996, the California State Board of Education granted waivers to four school districts which exempted them from complying with the Bilingual Education Act, permitted them to undo their bilingual education programs, and allowed them to create "sheltered English immersion" programs to replace students' native languages with English as quickly as possible. In Quiroz et al vs. State Board of Education (1997), the plaintiffs asserted that school district waivers allowing English-only instruction violated the rights of LEP (Limited English Proficient) students when they sued the Orange Unified School District in the California State Court's Sacramento location. In 1998, the judge ruled that the State Board of Education was not authorized to grant the waivers to school districts; and only federal laws, but not California state laws, applied to linguistic minority education.

<u>Findings of research regarding the effects of Proposition 227 on ELL education in California</u>
In 1998, Proposition 227 mandated that California schools use English Immersion methods with LEP students for one year and then transition them to mainstream classes. In 2000, California's Department of Education hired independent researchers to study the effects of Proposition 227 over five years. The researchers pointed out that California does not have statewide longitudinal data available on student progress. However, they did use longitudinal data from the Los Angeles Unified School District. To this data, they added case studies based on site visits, written surveys, and telephone interviews. They reported finding "no conclusive

evidence favoring one instructional program over another." They found that students in English Immersion and those in Bilingual Education had comparable academic progress. The 1984 reauthorization of the Bilingual Education Act defines LEP persons as persons not born in the United States; persons whose native language is not English; persons whose environments do not have English as the dominant language; and Native American groups that commonly use languages other than English.

Proposition 227
Proposition 227 was the culmination of a movement against bilingual education in California. In 1967, using languages of instruction other than English was legalized there, transitional bilingual education programs were authorized in 1974, and the Bilingual Education Act was reinforced in 1981 by more detailed definitions of school district responsibilities to linguistic minority students. However, this trend was reversed later in the 1980s by a governor who vetoed bilingual education laws and allowed the Bilingual Education Act to expire. This reversal was exacerbated in the 1990s by various state laws allowing schools to substitute English immersion for bilingual instruction despite a citizens'-rights lawsuit on behalf of LEP students and another governor's vetoing pro-bilingual law. Proposition 227 virtually outlawed all public-school bilingual education excepting certain special conditions, mandated English immersion for LEP students, and moreover limited English-immersion programs to one year, followed by mainstreaming.

Proposition 227 was passed in California in June 1998. This legislation basically prohibited bilingual education in that state's public schools, except under defined special circumstances. It required public schools in the state to place all limited English proficient (LEP) students in "sheltered English immersion" programs, requiring further that these programs last only one school year, after which students must be mainstreamed into English-speaking classes. In July 1998, in San Francisco U.S. District Court case Valeria G. vs. Wilson, an injunction against implementing Proposition 227 was requested but denied by the judge. The precedents cited for denial were set in the Supreme Court case Castañeda vs. Pickard (1981). These precedents permitted sequential programs that taught English first, subsequently teaching content subjects in English, resembling provisions of Proposition 227 for designing "structured English immersion" programs. A more favorable part of the judge's ruling involved obligating schools to compensate for any academic deficits incurred by LEP students while learning English within a reasonable time until they met grade/peer levels.

In 1999, the California State Board of Education adopted English Language Development (ELD) standards, which are aligned with the Content Standards for Language Arts and Reading. These standards furnish a structure for public school educators in designing instructional programs and in developing and procuring supportive teaching materials. These standards apply equally to all students, reinforcing Proposition 227's (1998) elimination of bilingual education programs and use of English immersion programs requiring linguistic minority students to develop English proficiency as quickly as possible. However, on the heels of Prop 227, a judge who refused an injunction against implementing it also ruled that schools were obligated to remedy any academic deficiencies in ESL students caused by English instruction to the temporary exclusion of content instruction. Therefore schools also can use the state standards to fulfill their obligation to ESL students through program designs and materials that help assure English proficiency. Founded on the 1996 Escutia Bill, the state also sponsored development in 1999 of an ELD test conforming to its ELD standards.

The passage of Proposition 227 virtually had eliminated bilingual education programs in California. While a U.S. District Court judge had refused an injunction not to implement Proposition 227, he also had ruled that public schools must make up for any academic losses to linguistic minority students while they were being taught English without content subject instruction. Previously, the re-designation of students from limited English proficiency (LEP) to fluent English proficiency (FEP) had been established and regulated first by Federal law in the Supreme Court case of Illinois vs. Gómez (1987) and then by California state law in the 1974 Chacón-Moscone Bilingual-Bicultural Education Act. However, in 1999, the California State Board of Education removed these reclassification provisions. Instead, it assigned each of the state's >1100 school districts the responsibility to set its own criteria for re-designating LEP students as FEP, making this process locally determined rather than regulated by Federal or State laws.

Bilingual education programs commonly offered in the United States

One bilingual education program is (English) Submersion/Immersion: LEP students are placed in regular/mainstream English-speaking classrooms and "sink or swim," i.e. they do not learn English and succeed academically, or they do. In ESL (English as a Second Language) or "pull-out" programs, students attend regular/mainstream classrooms most of the time, but are "pulled out" for short periods for special English instruction. In Transitional bilingual programs, students are instructed in both their native language (L1) and English, but the aim is to develop their English-language proficiency and phase out L1s as soon as possible. In Structured Immersion, teachers are fluent in the students' L1s, but speak and teach primarily in English. In two-way/bilingual immersion, elementary school students are taught in both the languages, beginning with mainly L1 and progressing to half L1-half English, with the goal of equal proficiency in both. In Developmental/Maintenance/Late-Exit Transitional programs, bilingually fluent instructors teach content subjects in both languages; transitions to mainstream classrooms are gradual, with some ongoing L1 support.

Myths related to bilingual education that have persisted over time

One educational myth asserts that creoles (languages evolved from combining languages) cannot be instructional languages since they are not true/legitimate languages. Any language can be used in instruction, given fluent teachers. A related myth asserts that anyone fluent in a language can teach it, but teacher preparation and experience are required beyond linguistic fluency. Also related is the myth that training teachers and developing materials in multiple languages is cost-prohibitive in multilingual countries. However, researchers find that aside from one-time start-up costs, expenses are similar in innovative vs. traditional programs. Furthermore, improved learning, educational time, graduate earning potentials, and school system savings add benefits. Another myth states in that in order to develop the greatest proficiency in English or any second language (L2), students must spend the most time being taught in that L2. However, research finds students' L1 instruction and proficiency promotes L2 proficiency, as well as student identity and self-confidence. It is a myth that for all multilingual nations, only one solution exists for beginning literacy and content instruction. In fact, many potential solutions exist.

Local and global ethical issues related to bilingual education

One issue relative to bilingual education is the central motivation around which debates revolve. Some policymakers and others may be motivated primarily by cultural dominance. As an example, many object to bilingual education on the grounds of preserving national and cultural identity. This objection occurs in the United States and other countries. Nonetheless, ultimately what is best for the students, including instructional approaches and methods that best promote their success in school and society, is a preferable motivation for such discussions. Another issue is the manner in which schools measure ESL students' progress. Because English-speaking Americans generally design American test instruments, many such instruments are consciously and/or unconsciously culturally biased, giving advantages to students with fluency in standard English. As humans become more globally interdependent, language as a means of understanding other peoples represents another issue. Also, as communications media have adopted English as a worldwide standard, the vanishing of minority languages is a consideration. Finally, American attitudes against learning other languages interfere with American knowledge and understanding of world matters.

Generalizations about language education

Research findings from various world educational settings indicate that academic/school language differs markedly from home language everywhere. In all settings, developing cognitive-academic language takes considerable time, i.e. 4-7 years of formal instruction. Students in all places learn cognitive and literacy skills and master academic content subject matter most easily when these are taught in languages familiar to the students. Once students have developed cognitive-academic linguistic skills, these skills easily transfer to other languages, as does their knowledge of school content subjects. Among all predictive factors, the relative degree of cognitive-academic language proficiency that a student develops in a second language is predicted best by that student's level of cognitive-academic language proficiency in his or her first language. An additional universal generalization found is that depending on their cultures, social groups, and

- 15 -

individual personalities, children learn second languages in different ways. These findings support additive bilingualism, wherein instruction includes languages familiar to students.

Common aspects promoting access to academic subject content

In all instructional programs that promote linguistic and academic content proficiency in multiple languages, the involvement and support of parents and communities is vital. In all successful school programs, educators encourage first-language (L1) development both to promote students' cognitive development and to provide a foundation for learning the second language (L2). Another factor in effective educational programs is that regardless of whether the language of instruction is a teacher's first or second language, the teacher demonstrates high levels of proficiency in comprehending, speaking, and utilizing the language of instruction. Teachers in such effective programs also have good preparation and training, knowledge of content subject matter, and cultural competence. Furthermore, they continually update and add to their preparation. Across nations, school systems, and programs, more effective programs do not cost more than traditional ones after start-up. In addition, the benefits of innovative bilingual educational programs outweigh the costs.

Transferring "cycles of discovery"

Educational researchers of bilingualism have examined various school programs in different countries. One important conclusion relates that a single bilingual education model cannot be adopted everywhere. Another conclusion asserts that educators need not be compelled to try applying a Western model in non-Western countries. Instead, a focus on more general processes determines the success of language education. Such fundamental processes include evaluation and its stages, forming hypotheses, building theories, experimenting to test the hypotheses and theories, and additional evaluation. These more general processes need to be transferred across different national, cultural, and social contexts in order to find the most suitable programs for each specific setting. That many policymakers identify bilingual education as "high-risk" attests to the complex interactions of linguistic, social, economic, political, and educational variables involved in selecting programs. Second-language/L2 skill thresholds for formal instructional applications vary markedly across content subjects, and all demand more than merely learning/communicating in L2s.

Considerations for educators, administrators, and parents

Parents, educators, and administrators must address their respective areas explicit and implicit goals for students' formal education. Stakeholders also should determine whether their region's population generally is satisfied with its students' levels of educational accomplishment, including both students who elect to pursue post-secondary studies and those who choose to stop after or during high school.

They should consider whether the area is linguistically and culturally homogeneous or heterogeneous. Relative to that consideration, they should discuss how bilingual education might complement their community's particular linguistic and cultural aspects. Involved and interested parties should ascertain whether there are policies—explicit or implicit—in their community relative to the part language plays in education. Also, they should find out whether such policies result from traditions or have been formed through planning language education. Then they should consider whether or how bilingual education would fit with their current policies.

Importance of a native language

Many people still believe that introducing another language into a school curriculum requires students to relearn concepts they have already mastered. However, plenty of solid educational research disproves this belief. On the contrary, once children develop basic knowledge of literacy, numeracy, and scientific discourse concepts in their first language, they can transfer this knowledge readily to any second, third, and additional languages that they may learn. Such research findings are further supported by the practical teaching experiences and observations of educators. There is always room for discovering more about the techniques, strategies, contexts, and constructs that help or interfere with transferring across languages the skills for interpersonal communication, which are contextualized; and the skills for cognitive and academic language applications, which are decontextualized. However, researchers find no question that these skills are transferable. Scholars conclude that cultivating a child's first language is crucial, both per se and to enable transfer to other languages.

Possibility and progress of worldwide multilingual education and literacy

The World Bank reported (1995) on top priorities and methods to improve educational development in the 21st century. One issue identified that not much is known about the status of various languages or their respective distributions, i.e. which people speak which languages, within many countries. World Bank employees encountered this issue during preliminary educational missions. They found that their lack of information about a country's languages precluded any valid instructional planning. Furthermore, many languages in the world are oral and have not been put into writing. Such languages equally have not been codified or elaborated upon. In many world countries, instructional materials do not exist either for beginning literacy or more advanced learning. Compounding the situation is that no teachers are trained to instruct students in many native languages. In order for global multilingual proficiency to develop, educational reform at a systemic level is needed; this reform is not possible without first addressing such issues as those mentioned here.

Considerations significant for parents, educators, and school administrators

Considerations include determining the priorities a community assigns to the ability of languages to promote national identity and cohesion; education's value for students who end their formal instruction earlier; and developing permanent, functional literacy with broad bases. Stakeholders also must consider whether the languages they teach have been committed to writing, codifying, standardizing, and elaborating; this consideration will affect, and even can prevent useful instructional planning. Planners for multilingual education also should consider whether their schools fully have developed curricula for all stages and levels of formal education. Curricula should include structures with specific objectives for affective, cognitive, content, and language learning; associated and/or illustrative methods and activities; and written materials supporting these objectives. Program planning should address whether teachers and students will have enough core and reference materials in languages to be taught, or whether professionals are available to develop such materials. Also, whether enough well-qualified teachers are fluent in target languages and trained to teach those languages is important.

Main conclusions from global research on the benefits of bilingual education

As researchers reported for UNICEF (1990), although language occupies a central part in children's developmental progress, the planning of young children's environments seldom focuses foremost on language. Nonetheless, the quality of children's language education urgently needs attention in light of the predominance of multilingualism in our modern world. Global longitudinal research shows that an individual given opportunities to attain high bilingual proficiency enjoys far greater benefits—economically, socially, cognitively, and personally—than an individual allowed to develop proficiency in only one language. Researchers conclude that educators should engage a variety of stakeholders in all parts of planning and implementing language education programs and avail themselves of all community resources for such planning and implementation. Educational researchers advise that in addition to carefully planning and implementing clearly defined courses of study, educators must employ committed, well-trained teachers and start innovational programs for bilingual/multilingual proficiency as early as feasible. Programs should prepare students to participate in our progressively globalizing economy by helping them develop social sensitivity, cultural richness, and linguistic competence.

U.S. legislations passed in the decade between 1964 and 1974

In the Civil Rights Act of 1964, Title VI banned discrimination in federally funded programs. Essentially, Title VI of the Civil Rights Act said all students have the right to effective and meaningful instruction and thereafter was cited frequently in other court cases. Title VII of the Elementary and Secondary Education Act (ESEA) of 1968, and of its 1974 reauthorization, also called the Bilingual Education Acts, allocated supplementary funds for school districts to create programs for meeting the recognized "special educational needs" of many students in the United States identified with limited English proficiency (LEP). On May 20, 1970, the Department of Health, Education, and Welfare (HEW) issued a Memorandum interpreting the regulations of this Title VII to outlaw schools' refusing access to any educational programs based on LEP status. The 1974 Equal Educational Opportunity Act defined the denial of equal educational opportunity, including an agency's failure to "take appropriate action to overcome language barriers that impede equal participation by students in an instructional program."

Civil Rights Language Minority Regulations of 1980

The Civil Rights Language Minority Regulations of 1980 stipulated bilingual instruction be delivered by qualified teachers and that bilingual education consist of four essential ingredients: identification, assessment, services, and exit. These regulations established the sequence of procedures still followed today by schools relative to providing educations for linguistic minority students.

Castañeda vs. Pickard (1981)

The U.S. Supreme Court's decision in Castañeda vs. Pickard (1981) established the standard used by the Courts for the examination of educational programs provided by schools for students with limited English proficiency (LEP). The ruling stipulated that school districts must have (1) a "pedagogically sound" educational plan for LEP students; (2) enough staff qualified to implement this plan, which included both training their currently employed teachers and hiring new, qualified teachers; and (3) a system in place for assessing the program's effectiveness. The wording of this decision did not require specifically "bilingual education" programs, but programs that took "appropriate action to overcome language barriers" to LEP students' educational participation.

14th Amendment to the U.S. Constitution

The 14th Amendment to the United States Constitution was adopted in 1868 as one of the Reconstruction Amendments after the Civil War. The passage of this amendment gave a constitutional foundation to the educational rights of linguistic minority. It guarantees that no U.S. State can pass or enforce any law that limits the immunities or privileges of its citizens; that no State can deny any person life, liberty, or property without following due law process; and that no State can refuse equal protection by laws to any citizen.

Brown vs. Board of Education (1954)

The 1954 case of Brown vs. Board of Education overruled the 1896 decision in Plessy vs. Ferguson that allowed "separate but equal" education for black students. In Brown vs. Board of Education, the Court ruled segregated public schools unconstitutional and ordered their desegregation. The opportunity for a public school education was declared a right "which must be made available to all on equal terms."

Lau vs. Nichols (1974)

In San Francisco, CA, a child of Chinese immigrants was failing in school because he could not understand the lessons, which were taught only in English. An attorney sued on the family's behalf. While lower courts decided against the plaintiffs, appeals to higher courts led to a class-action suit before the Supreme Court on behalf of nearly 1,800 Chinese parents with children struggling in English-only classes due to limited English-language proficiency (LEP). The Court decided that simply having the same schools, teachers, classes, and textbooks did not constitute equal treatment for LEP students because they were prevented meaningful education by not understanding English. Moreover, the justices ruled that making basic English skills a prerequisite for participation in educational programs was "to make a mockery of public education" because "Basic English skills are at the very core of what public schools teach...." In 1975, the Department of Health, Education, and Welfare (HEW) issued guidelines for schools regarding LEP students. These so-called "Lau Remedies" were ended by President Reagan's administration in the 1980s.

1980s U.S. Supreme Court decisions related to the examination, monitoring, and evaluation of public schools' educational programs for LEP students

The U.S.'s State Departments of Education first were officially assigned the legal responsibility for monitoring public school districts' implementation of educational programs for LEP (Limited English Proficient) students through the decision in the case of Idaho vs. Migrant Council (1981). The case of Illinois vs. Gómez (1987) further specified this state responsibility to include setting and enforcing the minimum requirements implementing language remediation programs. This decision also established requirements for re-classifying LEP students as FEP, or Fluent English Proficient, when their English language proficiency has progressed to fluency. Two Supreme Court cases that used the earlier decision in Castañeda vs. Pickard (1981) to evaluate school districts' educational programs for LEP students were Denver vs. School District No. 1 (1983) and Teresa P. vs. Berkeley Unified (1987).

Highlights in the 20th-century legal history of bilingual education

California has the largest proportion of linguistic minority students in the United States, making the legal history of its bilingual education significant to the entire nation. In 1967, Governor Ronald Reagan signed SB 53, overturning an 1872 law mandating English-only instruction and permitting California's public schools to use other instructional languages. In 1974, transitional programs of bilingual education were established through the Chacón-Moscone Bilingual-Bicultural Education Act. These programs adhered to the Federal guidelines for identifying and placing LEP

(Limited English Proficient) students and for re-designating LEP students as FEP (Fluent English Proficient) when they attained fluency. In 1981, the Bilingual Education Act was strengthened by the explicit, detailed specification of public school districts' responsibilities to LEP students. However, in 1986 Governor Deukmejian vetoed a bill to legalize bilingual education. In 1987 he vetoed a reauthorization bill, thereby permitting the Bilingual Education Act to expire. Even without the legal mandate, California public school districts continued enforcing the Chacón-Moscone Bilingual-Bicultural Education Act for nearly another decade.

Nations that successfully implemented L2 (second language) immersion programs in their schools

In the city of Saint-Lambert, in the province of Québec, Canada, across from Montreal, a large-scale immersion program was implemented in 1969 in the city's schools to teach English-speaking children French, the predominant language spoken there. Research studies have documented this program very well. Students speaking only English were taught only in French by qualified teachers for their first three school years. That student achievement, in both French and content area subjects, was very good. Some educational researchers/experts since have advocated adapting Canada's French-language immersion program for English-language immersion programs in the United States, particularly in states with large ESL populations. Israel is another nation that has used immersion. Attaining statehood in 1947, as a society composed of immigrants, Israel had people coming from many different countries, speaking a great variety of languages. To enable school success and societal integration, Israel developed a Hebrew immersion model. Students achieved academic Hebrew fluency within one or two years with this model.

Assumptions underlying the philosophy of English-only instructional models for ESL students regarding the concepts of independence vs. dependence on a native language

Models of English-only instruction for ESL students assume that using English exclusively has no potential for harm and moreover confers advantages to students in English-speaking schools and educational programs. Proponents of this philosophy find that ESL students are only hampered by using their native languages when they are attending English-speaking schools in America. Educators who support this perspective believe also that using the student's native language results in and perpetuates a "cycle of native language dependency," and that using English-only teaching is necessary in order to break this cycle. Those who advocate using English-only instructional models in public schools recommend in addition that the parents of ESL students should be encouraged to speak English, and only English, with their children in their homes.

Convergent research

When multiple lines of research come together, or converge, onto the same or similar results, convergent evidence exists. When investigators create research designs that purposively apply multiple theoretical approaches to study research questions, problems, or topics, they are conducting convergent research. Convergent research applies to the area of bilingual education, for example, to determine the best teaching practices to use in educating ESL students in America. One way investigators determine these best practices is by collecting data on academic achievement across schools, districts, and states, via scores reported on standardized school achievement tests. They can compare the scores of ESL/ELL students in different types of English instructional programs to see whether any patterns emerge indicating some types of approaches, methods, and programs as more effective than others. If ESL student achievement is better across many demographics, schools, regions, states, etc. wherever certain teaching practices are used, then the results converge on a group of practices, which researchers may conclude constitute best instructional practices with English language learners.

Language Acquisition and Development

Philosophical assumptions of bilingual education models for ESL students regarding the concept of depending on a native language (L1) vs. English-only instruction

Bilingual education models' philosophies differ from English-only instructional models' philosophy of avoiding L1 dependency. Bilingual education models assume everyone's dependence upon language to communicate. These models assert that native English speakers never are described as dependent on English. Therefore, these models find that ESL students profit from L1 instruction. The bilingual-education philosophy finds that viewing L1 use as dependency devalues speakers of languages other than English. This philosophy assumes that such denigration of people's language and culture can cause deep harm to students. The concerns of parents of ESL students about how English-only programs inhibit their children's expression during their initial school years is another rationale for this philosophy, as such constraints are equated with denying linguistic minority students equal educational opportunities. This philosophy also assumes that a benefit of bilingual education programs is that they forge connections between the school and the home, and these connections improve the students' learning.

Bilingual education models vs. English-only instructional models

Bilingual education models assume that both the student's native language (L1) and English should be languages of instruction at different times and for different reasons. This model assumes both languages as equally important. What ESL/ELL students learn in L1 is not viewed as only the means to the end of learning and using

English, but as a significant and valid end unto itself. Bilingual education models assume that the development of literacy skills in L1 mitigates chances of reading failure in both languages; that L1 uses speeds and improves content subject knowledge; and that the bi-literacy yielded by two-language instruction is an added benefit. English-only instructional models view being/becoming bilingual as an impediment to learning English as efficiently as possible and therefore as harmful to students' short-term and long-term scholastic achievement. This type of model finds it important to develop literacy and content subject knowledge only in English and assumes that second-language learners should only be instructed in English in our public schools.

Assumptions of English-only instructional models with bilingual education models in their assumptions about what determines how much English ESL students learn, and about learning academic content subjects in English vs. the native language (L1)

English-only models assume that one year of intensive instruction teaches ESL students enough English for mainstreaming into regular classes. Bilingual models assume that ESL students learn conversational English in 1-3 years, but academic English for complex and abstract tasks in content subjects takes 5-7 years in school settings. English-only models assume the time spent using English academically determines how much English ESL students learn. Bilingual models assume that exposure to English plus suitable teaching methods influence the amount of comprehensible input ESL students receive, which in turn determines how much English they learn. As a result, available comprehensible input is expanded by ESL students' content knowledge in their L1s, helping their English learning and academic progress. English-only models, however, assume that even students with low English proficiency can comprehend regular classroom instruction in English, given some teacher modifications. In this philosophy, the fastest English learning enables mainstreaming and promotes academic success.

Preserving the native language and culture vs. complete assimilation into the American culture and English language

Supporters of English-only instructional models find English proficiency the key to success both in school and in American society. They believe that in order to achieve complete assimilation into American culture and become true Americans, ESL students must forsake their native languages for English and their native cultures for American culture. Supporters of bilingual education models agree that English proficiency is a critical need, but also that it is only one of several variables contributing to academic success in America for ESL students. Another of these variables is being bilingual, according to advocates of bilingual education models. They find that in addition to enhancing school success, bilingualism enriches many domains of knowledge beyond what is available to monolingual students. As our economy becomes progressively more globalized and more competitive, bilingual education proponents believe that cultivating individual and group linguistic resources will benefit society, overall.

Bilingual education models regarding the merits of employing monolingual vs. bilingual English-speaking teachers in schools

Proponents of English-only instructional models for ESL students find monolingual English-speaking teachers just as qualified as bilingual English-speaking teachers when either are native English speakers. They believe monolingual native English-speaking teachers are even more qualified than bilingual teachers because they are always native English speakers. Furthermore, they find teachers' being monolingual in English forces ESL students to communicate with the teachers only in English. They also think "some" study of another language is sufficient for teachers to understand the challenges of second-language learning. Proponents of bilingual education concede monolingual teachers can be effective second-language instructors with proper training, but they find bilingual/multilingual teachers' proficiency in more than one language gives them higher levels of skills in language instruction. They find that such teachers' abilities to understand and communicate with ESL students improve learning; their greater metalinguistic awareness allows them to facilitate cross-linguistic transfer by teaching language comparisons/contrasts; and they offer students excellent bilingual and bicultural role models.

Transfer of knowledge across languages

Bilingual education models find the research studies into cross-linguistic transfer theory as sufficiently numerous and scientifically valid and reliable, whereas English-only instructional models find such theories unproven as valid. Proponents of English-only models assume that bilingual education theory claims transfer to another language only occurs after 3-5 years of native-language instruction. However, proponents of bilingual education models maintain that transfer does not occur in a linear sequence but instead happens concurrently, with ongoing and reciprocal learning in both languages. English-only instruction advocates believe this method equally effective for literacy, or more so than bilingual instruction. Bilingual education advocates observe an underlying ability commonly shared by cognitive and linguistic skills; they find developing this ability improves proficiency in both languages. English-only supporters believe that learning English faster enhances school success, and L1 reading instruction slows academic progress. Bilingual education supporters believe that students who read and write in L1 transfer their learning to English, thereby enhancing learning in both literacy and academic content..

Bilingual education models vs. English-only models as related to ESL students' self-esteem

Proponents of bilingual education find children's home languages integral to their identity formation. Furthermore, proponents find cultural identify an important part component of self-esteem. They find that experiencing failure at academic tasks because of inadequate English-language proficiency demoralizes ESL students. They believe that prohibiting or limiting native-language use in time will devalue students' native languages and cultures, eventually damaging their individual self-esteems, which in turn will damage their long-term levels of interest and progress in school. Advocates of bilingual education models believe that experiencing academic success in students' native languages will enhance their levels of self-esteem and promote their senses of academic self-efficacy, preparing them to approach learning English with a positive attitude. Proponents of English-only instruction do not believe that children's self-esteem is harmed by instruction exclusively in English. While they concede that ESL students' initial experiences being forced to use only English cause discomfort, they maintain that the positive experiences of learning English make up for this discomfort. They also find that learning English most quickly enhances school success.

Monolingual vs. bilingual educators

Proponents of English-only instruction for educating ESL students believe that educators who prefer this model are better equipped for decision-making relative to the education of linguistic minority students. Many proponents of English-only instruction feel that advocates of bilingual education models are influenced in their educational program planning by a bilingual philosophy, which English-only instruction advocates believe is misguided, or even by self-interest in promoting their chosen instructional approach. However, proponents of bilingual educational models believe that in our multicultural society, differences of opinion should not be used to create division and lack of trust between/among groups. They feel policies that exert authoritarian control or foster competition are counterproductive or even destructive in our heterogeneous culture. They urge collaboration and cooperation between monolingual and bilingual educators in school- and district-level program planning for second-language learning, which will benefit ESL students.

Perspectives on ESL student segregation of English immersion advocates and bilingual education advocates

Both English immersion and bilingual education advocates agree that segregation of ESL students is necessary and only temporary. However, English immersion proponents advise placing these students according to linguistic proficiency levels into heterogeneous native-language groups, while bilingual education advocates advise placing them in homogenous native-language groupings. Bilingual education supporters believe such segregation requires parental consent, provided that parents see important educational benefits to native-language instruction. English-only supporters believe such segregation may be mandated by the state as the "default" program placement for LEP students through its approval via a majority vote. Where state law mandates this segregation for English immersion programs, the parents must secure waivers to have their children alternatively placed in bilingual programs or mainstream classrooms. Bilingual education advocates find that children in bilingual classrooms have a variety of English proficiency levels and can communicate with, teach, and learn from each other. In communities with existing segregation, they find bilingual classrooms particularly significant in reflecting the community's bilingualism.

Parental roles in ESL educational placement

English-only instruction advocates believe structured English-immersion programs are best for ESL children. Accordingly, they feel student placement in such programs should be mandatory or recommended to parents. English immersion proponents feel public school policies should discourage parents from requesting waivers to place ESL children in other educational programs. English immersion advocates regard school policies to use English-only immersion programs for ESLs as reflecting public policy, decided through the majority opinions of the voting public. They say parents of ESL students must defer to the authority of school officials practicing these policies. Bilingual education advocates feel parents must be offered the choice of all legally permitted language instruction programs. They assert that options must be offered according to available district staff and resources rather than politics or ideologies. Schools must inform parents of pros and cons of various programs and allow teacher consultations and advisement. Bilingual education advocates assert that parental choices for ESL children's education should be respected in a manner equal to the respect given to native English-speaking parents' wishes.

School programs for teaching English and academic content to ESL students

Any school's program(s) for ESL students should be based on a chosen theoretical instructional model, which should be expressed clearly in the curriculum plan and/or policy document. Schools should define a progressive order to their curriculum plan, identifying what they will teach ESL students at each grade level. Schools should have overall "master plans," including standards or benchmarks, to which they can refer to determine whether ESL students are making sufficient progress in accordance with the goals, objectives, expectations, and guidelines of the ESL instructional program. Schools should identify how they group ESL classes and whether these assignments are most suitable for students' language proficiency and academic content achievement levels. A school's program should fit its state's or district's standards for language arts and academic subjects. Schools should see that teachers have in-service training on curriculum implementation and that their lesson plans and teaching strategies realize the school's identified instructional model. Schools also should provide suitable support materials for teaching ELD, ESL reading, and supported/"sheltered" academic content.

Rapid English immersion vs. bilingual ESL instruction as related to dropout rates

Advocates of English-only immersion programs for linguistic minority students claim learning English early and quickly will lower dropout rates, particularly in Latino populations. They rationalize that students require strong English literacy skills and linguistic knowledge in order to succeed in higher elementary-school grades. Advocates of bilingual education programs find the educational process for ESLs is long-term, encompassing grades K-12. They believe that concentrating only on learning English in the early grades causes students unnecessary losses in academic content instruction, when they could be learning both English and academic content concurrently. Bilingual education proponents rebut English immersion proponents' claim that knowing English early will lower dropout rates, arguing that knowing English is only one of a number of variables that influence dropping out of school. They also cite statistics that more students are retained in/repeat grades in English-only immersion programs, raising dropout rates among those retained students. In addition, they say that that students with strong academic skills plus strong cultural identities tend to pursue school through to graduation.

Assessing the implementation of educational programs

Schools implementing educational programs for ESL students should select teachers who have had in-service training and/or pre-service preparation in the different instructional models and methods for teaching linguistic minority students, in regard to the students' development of both the English language and of academic subject content knowledge. Teachers also should be trained in methods and procedures of assessment for ESL students. Administrators should know how many of their teachers are bilingual in English, as well as their students' native languages. They also should know how many teachers have obtained certification or other teaching credentials in teaching linguistic minority students, e.g. Cross-Cultural Language and Academic Development (CLAD) or Bilingual, Cross-Cultural, Language and Academic Development (BCLAD) certificates. Additionally, public school administrators should determine how many hours of in-service training teachers have accrued in cross-cultural linguistic and academic development when they assign those teachers to instructional programs for linguistic minority students.

Monitoring and enhancing instructional programs for linguistic minority students

Public schools should identify which instruments they use to assess ESL students initially for program placement and evaluate these instruments' appropriateness. They should consider multiple measurements of language proficiency and academic achievement, cut-off scores, and other criteria for use in placing ESL students; and whether such criteria are based in sound theory about second-language learning and cognitive development in ESL students and on effective ESL instructional practices. As ESL students learn English, schools should monitor their progress by disaggregating and analyzing their testing and measurement data regarding individual student progress in English proficiency, length of time in the instructional program(s), the program type(s), and programs addressing academic deficits. School criteria for reclassifying students in proficiency and for program exit should be based on objective data and solid teaching principles. Timely application of these criteria for all ESL students is important. Schools should have follow-up plans after student program exit and procedures/processes for remedying post-program academic deficits and/or insufficient academic progress.

Assessing ESL students' English-language proficiency

In addition to administering standardized tests and rating scales, educators may evaluate the English language skills of ESL students by conducting language interviews. Through these interactions, educators can observe and record a student's English listening comprehension, available English vocabulary and its accurate application, skills with using correct spoken English sentence structure, and general ability to communicate through listening and speaking in English. In addition to interviews, educators also may use checklists to create a record of which English language competencies a student has attained and to what level each respective competency has been attained. Checklists help educators to break down ESL students' English proficiency into component areas; to identify individual students' relative strengths, weaknesses, and disparities within English proficiency among areas; and to assure they have not overlooked any components. Teachers also make informal observations in class. These observations may be made systematically and recorded; and/or not systematized or recorded.

Instruments used to assess students' English-language development progress
Among standardized assessment instruments used, LAS Links (CTB/McGraw-Hill) is an integrated group of instruments to assess ESL students for student program progress, program planning, and student placement. Various state school systems use the Idea Proficiency Test or IPT as an annual English-language proficiency test to comply with federal and state policies. The Bilingual Syntax Measure (BSM) assesses student proficiency with sentence structure in L1 and L2. The Basic English Skills Test (BEST) has been used to assess ESL students' general English proficiency levels, for monitoring as well as placement. The Comprehensive English Language Test (CELT) is a more extensive assessment. The Woodcock-Muñoz Language Survey (WMLS), testing student skills for surviving academically in Spanish and/or English, is used for program evaluation and monitoring as well as for program placement and exit. Some standardized tests focusing on specific modalities in English include the Test of Spoken English (TSE), the Listening Comprehension Test (LCT), and the Combined English Language Skills Assessment in a Reading Context (CELSA).

<u>Measures used to assess ESL student progress</u>

In addition to a variety of formal, standardized test instruments used to evaluate ESL student progress, educators use other means of assessing students' English progress in developing English language skills. For example, teachers may use rating scales based on their observations their ESL students, such as the Student Oral Language Observation Matrix or SOLOM. Teachers rate ESL students' linguistic performance in the five domains of vocabulary, listening comprehension, grammar, pronunciation, and fluency, through observing them in varied, ongoing school situations such as classroom discussions, interactions among different classes, social interactions, etc. They rate each domain on a five-point scale, and scores can be combined for an overall rating of oral English proficiency. The U.S. Foreign Service Institute (FSI)'s Interagency Language Roundtable (ILR) Scale is another measure, which identifies five language proficiency levels for communication: Elementary, Limited Working, Professional Working, Full Professional, and Native or Bilingual Proficiency.

Criteria educators use to place ESL students in appropriate instructional programs

ESL students are first given assessment instruments in order to determine their current levels of English-language proficiency. These initial proficiency scores help in deciding on appropriate student program placement. Educators also should give ESL students literacy assessments in their native languages (L1s), as their L1 literacy both will influence their L2 literacy and inform their initial program placements. To inform placement decisions, school personnel also should ascertain immigrant ESL students' educational histories in their original countries. Another criterion is which types of programs are available in the school. The types of groupings of various ESL students are additional criteria for deciding on program placements. Educators should consider the duration of time that an immigrant ESL student has been in the USA in placement decisions. They also should consider how long the student has been in an English-language instructional program when applicable. Administrators must take teacher-supplied information into account, as well as their school's staffing patterns, for program placement. Moreover, they must have the consent of ESL students' parents for placement.

Assessing ESL students' progress in academic content learning

One component of assessing academic progress involves standardized achievement tests, which are important because of their validity, or their effectiveness in testing what they are supposed to test; and their reliability, or the ability to reproduce similar results across repeated administrations. In addition to formal testing, teachers also use other criterion-referenced tests, which may be available commercially and/or created by the teachers. These tests compare student performance to predetermined criteria for the student's grade or age level in the specific academic content areas. Because an ESL student's English-language reading skills affects the student's academic performance, teachers also may administer

- 29 -

informal reading inventories and/or use other reading assessment instruments such as the Consortium of Reading Excellence (CORE) assessment, the Leveled Reading Skills Competencies Test, the Qualitative Reading Inventory, and etc. Teachers also may obtain writing samples from ESL students, based and evaluated on a rubric of the teacher's choice. ESL students' grades also are used in assessing their academic progress.

Determining whether an ESL student is qualified to exit that program

Educators administer English-language proficiency tests to ESL students as initial measures of their skill levels in order to help determine the best programs and levels for their placement. These same tests may be re-administered after time in an instructional program; the student's progress is seen by comparing the re-test results to the initial test results. Improvement in re-test scores is one criterion for assessing an ESL student's readiness to exit the program and join mainstream classes. Another criterion used is a review of the student's current scores on standardized tests, both in English reading skills and in academic content subjects. Educators often also include informal reading inventories to assess the ESL student's current English-language reading level, both in general and in specific academic subjects. Educators also will test the ESL student's English writing proficiency in grammar, spelling, syntax, and composition. A student's duration in the program is another factor. The student's grades in language arts and academic subjects are considered, as are teacher recommendations. Parental consent is also needed for program exit.

Behaviorist, Cognitive, Nativist, and Interactionist theories of language acquisition

B. F. Skinner was the major proponent of the Behaviorist view of language acquisition, which holds that children develop language the same way that all organisms learn everything. Their early linguistic responses to environmental stimuli are reinforced selectively by adults; they will repeat rewarded responses, while ignored responses are less likely to persist. Jean Piaget was the major proponent of the Cognitive theory of language development. He viewed language acquisition as one component of a child's overall cognitive development; hence, he believed language develops following the same stages he proposed for all intellectual progress. Noam Chomsky is the major proponent of the Nativist or Innate theory of language development. He maintains that humans possess an internal Language Acquisition Device, allowing them to generate linguistic structures more easily and naturally than they could without it. Furthermore, Chomsky asserts that environmental factors influence, but do not determine, this process. Jerome Bruner was the main proponent of Interactionist theory, which says that interactions between the child and parents/caregivers determine the course of language development.

Piaget's Cognitive Developmental theory

Piaget viewed language acquisition as part of a child's overall cognitive development; therefore, according to Piaget, language acquisition follows the stages of intellectual development he proposed. Piaget stated that to acquire any specific linguistic form, a child first must be able to understand its underlying concept. Piaget defined the stages of cognitive development as Sensorimotor, Preoperational, Concrete Operations, and Formal Operations. Children in Sensorimotor and Preoperational stages cannot perceive others' viewpoints; Piaget dubbed them egocentric. Sensorimotor infants first perform reflexive activities, and then learn to coordinate their sensations and motor movements. As they become aware of objects, infants develop object-orientation and object permanence (realizing objects continue to exist when out of their sight), then intentional actions. Infants develop mental constructs (schemata) representing objects. By age 2, they internalize these schemata, thereby enabling symbolic thinking—representing things/concepts with linguistic symbols, i.e. words. Concrete Operations-stage children can perform and reverse mental operations, but only regarding concrete objects. In Formal Operations they grasp and manipulate abstract concepts, including abstract word meanings (semantics) and operations (higher-order syntax, grammar, etc.).

Noam Chomsky

LAD and Syntactic Theory
Chomsky's Language Acquisition Device (LAD) is his theoretical construct representing an innate mechanism or tool set he says all humans possess for learning language. He finds that in all languages, the Universal Grammar (UG) rules are the same. Therefore, he has stated that "all children share the same internal constraints which characterize narrowly the grammar they are going to construct" (1977). Chomsky asserts that since the brain is part of the body, the mental world is part of the biological world in which we live. As a result, the mental world follows biological processes. He designates language development as "language growth" in that the "language organ" grows in the brain like any other bodily organ. His Syntactic Theory explains that speakers understand internal sentence structure (syntax) via "phrase structure rules." His "poverty of stimulus" argument is that children hear many fragmented/ungrammatical/unstructured adult utterances, yet still construct correct grammars, which he views as evidence of universal, inborn language abilities. He also points out that children having different experiences still form the same linguistic rules.

Chomsky's theory of Innate language development
Chomsky proposed the "Innateness Hypothesis" that all humans have an inborn ability to develop language, in the form of what he called "Universal Grammar" (UG) or "Generative Grammar"—a set of linguistic rules with which our brains are pre-programmed. Chomsky says that this inherent blueprint or template for language structures explains why even deaf and/or blind children and/or children with deaf and/or blind parents develop language in the same ways, following the same stages,

as do all other children. Chomsky has stated that language development is an inevitable occurrence with children rather than a voluntary action. In other words, given a suitable environment, including "appropriate nutrition and environmental stimulation," they will acquire language naturally, similarly to their predetermined physical maturation processes. Chomsky's UG does not contain specific rules of every language. Instead, Chomsky's view asserts that general "principles and parameters" from which language rules are derived.

<u>Concept of transformations according to Chomsky's Transformational Grammar</u>
Noam Chomsky has proposed that language consists of "deep structures" and "surface structures." Deep structures are the forms in which linguistic concepts originate. He says our minds then perform "transformations" which change these deep structures to surface structures, which are the final forms of our spoken and written language. For example, a basic statement is a deep structure, and we transform it to make it grammatically complete. As a result, we turn the statement into a question or a negative, or both. A deep structure might convey "He is going out." Chomsky proposes that we automatically make transformations to this structure to turn it into a question: "Is he going out?" or a negative: "He is not going out;" or both: "He is not going out, is he?" So for Chomsky, the essential concept is the same, but the semantic changes, i.e. changes in meaning, and syntactic changes, i.e. changes in sentence structure that produce such variations as questions and negatives, are achieved through transformations from the same deep structure to various surface structures.

Skinner's Behaviorist theory

According to Skinner's theory of Operant Conditioning, learning is a function of change that occurs in an organism's observable behaviors. Behaviorists see language development as a process of building behaviors through conditioning that occurs through interactions with the environment. Skinner stated that adults selectively reinforce young children's vocalizations which to them resemble recognizable speech and disregard those vocalizations they find irrelevant. Children will repeat reinforced, i.e. rewarded, responses. The child's responses gradually become more similar to adult speech through what Skinner called successive approximations. Skinner believed children acquire verbal behavior matching that of their "given verbal community" via this process. As their vocalizations approach recognized speech forms, these "produce appropriate consequences" for the children. Main principles include that positively reinforced (rewarded) behavior recurs, that responses can be shaped through presenting information in small increments, and that reinforcement promotes response generalization to other similar stimuli. Limitations include that the rules and structure of language cannot be derived through sheer imitation, and that children often cannot repeat adult utterances.

Jerome Bruner

Interactionist theory of language acquisition
Bruner emphasizes adult-child interactions as promoting children's language acquisition. Bruner sees child-directed speech (CDS), i.e. the linguistic behaviors of adults in speaking to children, as having a specialized adaptation of supporting the process of language development. Bruner termed such support "scaffolding." The concept of scaffolding—support given to young learners as needed and gradually withdrawn as they develop more autonomy—has also been applied to Lev Vygotsky's sociocultural theory of learning, especially his Zone of Proximal Development (the distance between what a learner can do on his/her own and what s/he can do with guidance), and to Stephen Krashen's theory of ESL acquisition. Whereas Chomsky has proposed a universal Language Acquisition Device (LAD) we all possess, Bruner countered this proposal with a Language Acquisition Support System (LASS), which reflects Bruner's greater emphasis on the interactions of the learning child with the family and social environment and the support they give. Chomsky's LAD reflects innate structural ability; Bruner's LASS reflects innate social ability to interpret situations/interactions.

Significance of the concept of categorization
Bruner believes that the ability to categorize plays a highly important role in learning. He identifies perception, i.e. our brains' awareness and interpretation of sensory stimuli, as a form of categorization; our conceptualizing, i.e. formulating ideas, as a type of categorization; our actual learning as a process of forming categories; and our decision-making as also a kind of categorizing process. A key similarity between the theories of Piaget and Bruner is their shared belief that children have intrinsic abilities helping them to understand the world, and that their actively interacting with the environment promotes their cognitive development. A key difference between Piaget and Bruner is that Piaget focused on only the cognitive aspects of development and on the learner's interactions with/actions upon the environment, while Bruner focused more on the social aspects of learning and on the learner's interactions with parents and others. Among those social aspects is language, which Bruner stressed is important to cognitive development and represents one example of scaffolding or support.

Jerome Bruner related the social aspects of learning to language development
Bruner pointed out that children learn language within the social context of communication with their parents and other people. As children grow within this social setting, they need to communicate with their parents/caregivers in their environment. Bruner said that because of this necessity, children therefore imitate and gradually learn to take on the body movements and language of these adults. This necessity establishes both the reason and the method for children's language learning. Another linguist, McNamara, has interpreted Bruner's theory further to explain that unlike the Language Acquisition Device (LAD), an innate mechanism for learning language posited by Nativist linguist Noam Chomsky, Bruner's Language Acquisition Support System (LASS), an innate ability to read and interpret social

situations and interactions and hence to understand language and learn it readily, enables language acquisition in children. Bruner (1991) discussed the "narrative construction of reality," writing that our constructions of our personal ideas of reality are mediated by symbol systems including language and other "cultural products" including narrative or storytelling.

Constructivism as a theory of learning

Constructivist theory understands learning as a process in which learners actively build, or construct, new concepts and ideas upon their foundations of existing knowledge. Cognitive-developmental psychologist Jean Piaget often is credited with founding constructivist learning theory, and the work of Lev Vygotsky and Jerome Bruner, who both proposed socially-oriented theories of learning, have strongly influenced social constructivism. Bruner also posited three types and stages of development in children. Enactive representation is action-based and begins in a child's first 18 months; it is similar to Piaget's Sensorimotor stage of development in that the child learns through acting physically upon objects and observing the results. Iconic representation is image-based and develops after 18 months of age; children can then learn through observing pictures and models in addition to through actions. Piaget also theorized that children learn symbolic representation around the same age. Symbolic representation involves abstract thought without needing concrete objects. While Piaget believed this ability develops in the preteen years, Bruner believes it starts around age 6-7 years.

Scaffolding

Wood, Bruner and Ross (1976) concluded from their research that parents and other adults give children "scaffolding," or the temporary support they need to promote their cognitive growth. They found that in everyday interactions involving play, in order to help children understand new concepts and perform new tasks, adults provided support structures analogous to the scaffolds temporarily erected around buildings under construction. This analogy is consistent with the constructivist theory to which Bruner subscribed, wherein we construct our realities as well as new ideas based on our knowledge. The purposes of scaffolding include making new ideas or tasks simpler and easier for children to understand, giving learning children motivation and encouragement to learn, emphasizing the most important components of a task and/or any errors they may have made in attempting it, and supplying adult models for children of the behaviors they are engaged in learning, which the children can observe and then imitate.

First/native language acquisition in children

When children begin to speak, usually at around 12-18 months, they utter single words such as "Mama," "Dada," "doggie," etc. During this phase, the Holophrastic stage of language development, children holistically express concepts through single words until they are physically and cognitively able to utter multiple words.

Between the ages of 18 and 24 months, children typically begin to make two-word utterances in the Two-Word stage. These utterances are not sentences in a grammatical sense, but they represent "mini-sentences" semantically as they express relationships between the words and the things they represent: "Mommy milk" can mean "Mommy, I want milk;" "Daddy go" could mean "Daddy went to work," "Daddy is going somewhere," or "I want to go with Daddy," etc. Some two-word sentences at this stage are also grammatical or more easily understood, e.g. "Watch this!", "Good food," etc. In the Telegraphic stage, children aged 24-30 months utter 3-4 word sentences, which often are still ungrammatical, but understandable. Children aged 2-4 years and older speak in longer and eventually more complex sentences.

General views of linguists about learning a second language

Many linguists believe that children possess their maximal capacity to learn a second language until around the age of six years. They consider this time a "critical period" wherein children can learn up to five or six non-native languages most easily. Between the ages of six and seven years, linguistic researchers have found that children's ability to learn additional languages decreases slightly, but they are still quite able to learn other languages between the ages of seven and 11 years. Language learning ability, though somewhat less than the optimal capacity displayed during the critical period, continues to be good for children aged 12 to 17 years. Between the ages of 17 and 31 years, the ability of individuals to acquire new languages gradually diminishes further. While linguists historically have believed that adults' language-learning ability "almost ends" around age 30-31, adults still can learn new languages, albeit less naturally and with more effort than children. More recent innovations in learning techniques (e.g. Rosetta Stone) facilitate adult language learning.

Fundamental Difference Hypothesis

The Fundamental Difference Hypothesis states that learning a second language (L2) is different from learning a first language (L1). When babies first start to babble, they have been observed to be able to make the wide range of speech sounds found in all languages. For example, English-speaking babies may roll their /r/s as in Spanish. However, as adults selectively reinforce the vocalizations that sound like English words and those vocalizations become more like adult speech, children learning to speak English as their L1 lose this flexibility. For example, many adults and older children are no longer able to produce the rolled /r/ sound when they try to learn Spanish. Linguists hypothesize that acquisition of their L1 occupies the majority of children's linguistic faculties, reducing their openness to receiving and acquiring the features of different languages (L2, L3, L4, etc.). Another basic difference is that while learning any L1 is largely natural, even unconscious at times, learning any L2 requires more mental capacity, conscious attention, memory, effort, and even studying.

Interlanguage and fossilization in L2 learning

When students are learning a new, non-native language, some of the rules in their first and second languages will be the same or similar, while other rules will be markedly different. For example, the syntactic (sentence structure and word order) rules of German differ so much from those of English that sentences with the same meanings would have very different word orders in each language; but because English also retains parts of its Germanic origins, there are also similarities, e.g. in the morphology of many irregular verbs and in vocabulary. Because of influences from Latin and Latinate languages such as French and Spanish, although these languages differ phonologically from English, they share many cognate words, which facilitates translation and comprehension. However, when a student applies rules from another language that do not match English rules, interlanguage results: the student is speaking neither L1 nor L2/English but something in between. Some linguists/educators have found that uncorrected interlanguage features can become resistant to change and permanently entrenched in a learner's speech, which is called fossilization.

Research findings on learning English at different ages

A number of linguistic and educational researchers have examined the ease with which immigrants attain English language proficiency after coming to America. These researchers have found that the ages at which people arrive in America have definite influences on the degrees of proficiency attained by ESL learners. For example, Johnson and Newport found that people who had immigrated to the United States as children between three and eight years of age achieved scores on language tests equivalent to the scores attained by native speakers of English. However, those immigrants who had arrived in the United States between the ages of eight and 15 years achieved lower scores than both the native English speakers and the immigrants who had arrived at younger ages. These researchers also discovered that ESL learners between the ages of 17 and 31 years attained the lowest scores of all age groups they tested.

Abilities of adults and older children to learn a second language (L2)

Whereas typical children learn their native/first language (L1) easily and naturally, this is not the case for adults and older children learning a second language (L2), which requires the flexibility to learn linguistic features and patterns (phonological, morphological, grammatical, syntactic, and semantic) that differ from their L1. The abilities of adults to learn an L2 includes a broad range: some adults are quite gifted at learning new languages, others are average at learning them, and others have such difficulty in trying to learn an L2 that they completely fail at it. Unlike childhood L1 development, later L2 acquisition involves many more factors. Individuals who have grown up bilingual or multilingual find it easier to learn additional languages. Motivation is a significant factor: individuals with a greater need and/or desire to learn and use another language are more successful. The quantity and quality of linguistic input they receive and output they produce are also learning factors. Another is the individual's "sociolinguistic competence," which includes communicative, strategic, and grammatical competencies.

Development and Assessment of Literacy and Biliteracy

Content standards as they relate to student assessment

Content standards define the specific areas of knowledge every student needs to learn. These areas are usually the traditional subjects of English (or language arts), mathematics, science, social studies, music, art, and drama; some also include general concepts and interdisciplinary studies. Some reflect one grade level and specific academic content, while others combine grade levels and integrate the content across academic disciplines. Standards should not be so broad they cannot be used as instructional guidelines or to evaluate students effectively.

Specific standards are created by individual states and various national educational organizations; ideally, the groups work in tandem. The content standards should be a result of community meetings that include academic and business representatives so that the requirements of both are recognized and met. These meetings should be moderated by state leaders and open to the public so that everyone helps define what needs to be taught and the methods used to teach it.

Performance standards

Evaluating students' progress using performance standards is tricky because there is no clear definition of the term. Are the standards based upon test performance? If so, do they take into account test grading practices? Do they mean the method of reporting test scores, e.g., basic equates to unacceptable, proficient to adequate, and advanced to excellent? How good is good enough? The Goals 2000: Educate America Act says "performance standards means concrete examples and explicit definitions of what students have to know and be able to do to demonstrate that such students are proficient in the skills and knowledge framed by content standards." Performance standards must also be appropriate for the age, feasible to administer, and useful for evaluating progress. According to this definition, content and performance should be evaluated together in order to obtain a clear picture of the student's progress or lack thereof.

Technical quality of assessments

One issue that must be considered when developing academic assessments is the technical quality of the examination. The National Center for Research on Evaluation, Standards and Student Testing (CRESST) developed the following criteria to evaluate technical quality:

- Cognitive Complexity: requires problem-solving, critical thinking and reasoning ability.
- Content Quality: correct responses demonstrate knowledge of critical subject matter.
- Meaningfulness: students understand the value of the assessment and the tasks involved.
- Language Appropriateness: clear to the students and appropriate to the requested task.
- Transfer and Generalization: indicates ability to complete similar tasks and the results permit valid generalization about learning capabilities.
- Fairness: performance measurements and scoring avoid factors irrelevant to school learning.
- Reliability: consistently represents data added to students' background knowledge.
- Consequences: it results in the desired effect on students, instructors and the educational system.

Credibility and feasibility of student assessments

For any assessment method to be successful, it must be introduced to the community in a way that builds support rather than causing confusion, resentment, and skepticism. Parents, teachers, students, and the public need to understand the purpose of the assessment, what it is intended to accomplish, why it is necessary and how it will logically integrate with methods already in place. Allowing the community to review the test and try to answer some of the questions will usually help generate acceptance of the new tool.

Development, scoring and reporting costs, and teacher expectations should be considered before a new assessment is introduced and implemented. Sometimes the cost is prohibitive. Teachers may not be qualified to prepare students or to administer the test and training may not be available or affordable. These potential stumbling blocks need to be addressed before a new assessment is added to the existing requirements.

Articulation matrix and Bloom's taxonomy

An articulation matrix is the relationship between activities and outcomes. It is a defined set of goals and the methods used to reach them. For example in a graduation matrix, completing the required courses is the outcome, and the lectures, homework assignments, projects, papers, tests, and evaluations are the activities.

Bloom's Taxonomy, which is a hierarchical classification system, is an articulation matrix that outlines six levels of cognitive learning. At each step, students reach a predictable level of mastery:

- Knowledge Level: ability to define terms.
- Comprehension Level: finish problems and explain answers.
- Application Level: recognizes problems and uses methods to solve them.
- Analysis Level: ability to explain why the process works.
- Synthesis Level: can use the process or part of it in new ways.
- Evaluation Level: can create different ways to solve problems and use designated criteria and can select the best method to obtain the correct solution.

Assessment station

An assessment station is a designated area, inside or outside of the classroom, used for the specific purpose of evaluating students' progress performing a task. Individuals or groups can be assigned to complete a task, use a piece of lab equipment or work with some technological device. The purpose is to assess the knowledge acquired, processes used, skills displayed, and general attitude about the task, and if working in a group, how each student interacts with the other members of the team.

The assessment station should function the same way every time it is used. This builds consistency and reduces the time needed for explanations and demonstrations before and during future assessments. Instructions should be clear, concise and specific and explain exactly how the area should be left for the next student. Activities performed in the assessment station should be simple, straightforward and relate to the material being studied.

Because the assessment station is an interactive tool, the area needs to be equipped with the appropriate equipment necessary to complete the task. If the activity is an experiment, the area needs to be ventilated and appropriate safety precautions taken, e.g., having water available and a fire extinguisher at hand. The students need to understand how to operate the instruments in a safe manner and therefore instructions should be provided both in writing and verbally. Questions should be asked and answered before any activity is started. If it is a group activity, each student needs to contribute to the assigned task.

The work submitted by each student is evaluated using a rating/grading scale or a checklist. For example if the task required the use of a microscope, the checklist should have points related to its use. If it was a group project, cooperation, helpfulness and leadership skills should be noted.

Individual assessments

Individual assessments focus on the progress each student made during a defined period of time (e.g., every six weeks, at the end of the semester) rather than in a team collaboration. A variety of activities such as written assignments, oral presentations, and class participation should be incorporated into the assessment in order to obtain a broader, more realistic view of the student's understanding of the material. The assessment process should be fully explained so that the student knows what is expected. He is evaluated using one or all of the following standards:

- self-referenced —based on his previous level of progress
- criterion-referenced — a defined, school or district-wide standard
- norm-referenced — based on the progress of groups of students the same age or grade level

Using a combination of standards instead of relying on one method presents a clearer, more accurate picture of the student's growth.

Individual assessments are easily understood by students and parents and mesh with most school districts' systems. Because each student is evaluated based on criteria established by state performance and/or content standards, it is easy to measure the success of department curricula. Self-referenced standards provide feedback about the student's strengths and weaknesses. They can help motivate the student to work harder and take more responsibility for his learning. Students sometimes set personal goals and expectations. Individual assessments help them measure their success. These evaluations provide the teacher insight into any special help the student might need.

Individual assessment can create and encourage a very competitive environment in which some students are unable to compete effectively. It makes it difficult to evaluate students' ability to work with a team and judge their interaction with others both of which are important to the educational experience. They can also be also very time consuming for the teacher to complete fairly and accurately.

Group assessments

Group assessments focus on how students cooperate and collaborate in completing a project assigned to the group rather than to a single student. The same activities used in individual assessments are used, such as written assignments, oral presentations, and group participation, but they are used to evaluate social and interactive skills as well as the work produced. The students' willingness to accept being evaluated for a group project is based on if and how long they have been exposed to this type of cooperative collaboration and if they feel the grading system is applied fairly. If this project is the first time students in a competitive environment are expected to work together, there may be some misunderstandings and objections about what is expected, how it works, and how each student will be evaluated. It is critical the teacher explains the evaluation process clearly, answers questions, addresses reservations, and closely monitors individual contributions as well as the progress of the project.

There are three ways to evaluate a group project: group grade only, individual grade only, or a combination of both. The reason for group projects is to teach cooperation in a team environment. Giving everyone the same grade can foster some degree of esprit de corps. It also frees the teacher from having to decide who was responsible for what part of the project. A group grade, however, can cause resentment, especially if students are not used to working in a group and are used to earning grades based on a competitive scale. Students understand individual grades, but in a group project environment the competitive scale diminishes the spirit of cooperation because everyone is working for himself rather than for the good of the team. Giving a group grade and an individual grade addresses both issues. Basing eighty percent of the grade on cooperation and collaboration and twenty percent on individual production recognizes the importance of working for the group and the necessity of individual contributions.

Performance contracts

A performance contract is a written agreement between an individual student or a group of students and a teacher about a specific activity. The assignment can be a research paper, an oral presentation with props, or some other project. The contract clearly states the goal, explains the activity, establishes a timeline, and describes who will do what and how it will be done. Sometimes the agreement also details the criteria to be used to evaluate the finished product. This tool helps students learn to plan a project by breaking it into manageable parts and shows them how to utilize their time more efficiently. Not only can the completed project be graded, but the performance contract itself can be evaluated. The teacher should assess the student's participation in setting up the contract, his willingness to compromise when necessary and his general attitude about the concept and the process.

Performance contracts can be a great learning experience for students by teaching them how to plan and prioritize and encouraging them to avoid procrastination. However, some students may have trouble understanding the concept, so it may be necessary to review the planning, organizing, and writing steps several times before they are able to grasp the idea. Using contracts can also help a struggling student in other areas of his life. These agreements can be developed to address attendance requirements and expected behavior standards or to plan weekly or monthly homework schedules.

If a teacher has never used performance contracts, he needs to understand that setting up the system and helping the students write their agreements is very time consuming, especially in the beginning. It can help, as a class project, to create a performance contract based on a completed project. This strategy sometimes reduces the learning curve for all the students.

In order for a performance contract to be a learning experience, the guidelines for writing one should be very general. The teacher can either give the student a written list of suggestions or, preferably, discuss them one-on-one. Some questions that might be used:

- What work items are you planning to include?
- Where you will find the necessary data: Personal reference books, the internet, the library? Do you have additional sources?
- How long will it take to outline a plan, research the topic, and finish the project?
- What criteria should be used to evaluate the finished product?

Questions that might be used to evaluate the completed contract:

- Is the contract realistic relative to required completion date?
- Are the contract questions appropriate to the project objectives?
- Were reliable and appropriate sources chosen?
- How comprehensive is the plan?
- Does the student understand his capabilities and recognize his limitations?

Form to use when asking for student feedback about a group project

---

Rating For Group Project

Student Name: _____

Date of Project _____ to _____

Circle the phrase that describes how you feel.
Choosing the members of your group:
I really like it.　　　　　**It's okay.**　　　　　**I don't like it.**
Having the teacher choose group members:
I really like it.　　　　　**It's okay.**　　　　　**I don't like it.**
The group deciding how you are going to complete the project?
I really like it.　　　　　**It's okay.**　　　　　**I don't like it.**

Comments:

_____

_____

_____

Portfolio

A portfolio is a collection of the student's work assembled over a period of time (e.g., six week grading period, one semester, the entire year). Various items can be included: contracts, copies of completed activities such as papers; presentations and pictures of props; performance assessments made by the student, his peers, and the teacher; copies of class work and homework; classroom tests; and state-mandated exams. A portfolio is a powerful aide in assessing the student's progress and an excellent format to present to parents so they can review their child's progress. The decision on what to include should be a collaboration between the student and the teacher. What will be included: examples of best work, worst work, typical work, or perhaps some of each? Will the student keep a copy as a reference point? Decisions need to be made and rules established as early as possible in the process so that progress is accurately and fairly recorded.

Once decisions have been made about what will be included, it is important to begin with baseline data for comparison as the portfolio grows. Selected material can be placed in a folder or large envelope with the student's name on the front. Each addition needs to be dated with an explanation attached stating why the item was included and what features should be noted. Teachers who use portfolios will often create assignments with the intention of including it in the package. As the contents grow, it may become necessary due to space limitations to review the items and remove some daily work, quizzes, or tests. Once the portfolio is complete, the teacher needs to have a method to evaluate the contents and review the student's progress in areas such as creativity, critical thinking, originality, research skills, perseverance, responsibility, and communication effectiveness. A checklist can be useful (see card 192).

Self-assessment and peer-assessment

Self-assessment allows the student to become involved in the evaluation process. He takes more responsibility for the learning process because he is expected to reflect upon his attitude about and attention to assigned activities and the product produced. To be truly effective, the student should be involved in developing the evaluation criteria. It gives him more control. Instead of the teacher having all of the power and being perceived as such, some power shifts to the student in allowing him to help determine the rating scale used, to participate in evaluating the finished product, and to provide direct input into the grade which he receives.

During peer-assessments, students learn by listening to other students critique their work and make suggestions on ways to improve it. The student doing the evaluation must think analytically about their peer's work product; in doing so, it should help him become more critical about his own work. Teachers need to moderate these discussions and stress consistency, being descriptive and not judgmental, realistic, positive, and reflective.

Work products and response groups

Work Products are completed assignments that are evaluated on the basis of the topic chosen as well as creativity, originality, organization, understanding of the subject matter, social and academic progress, and success in meeting and/or exceeding predetermined criteria along with any other items deemed important by the individual teacher. Work products can take many different forms, including but not limited to research papers, poems, fiction and non-fiction stories, bulletin boards, video and audio tapes, computer and laboratory demonstrations, dramatic performances, debates and oral presentations, paintings, drawings and sculptures, and musical compositions and performances. **Response Groups** are discussions about a particular subject. Frequently, the students themselves start them spontaneously in response to a shared experience. They want to talk about the event because it affected all of them in some way. Teachers can gain insight into the students' critical thinking skills, information and observations shared, willingness to participate in the discussion and behavior within the group.

Performance contract that can be used for any subject

Student's Name: _____

Teacher's Name: _____

Contract Dates: _____

Purpose of Contract: _____

I am planning a study of: _____

Reason for choosing this topic: _____

Main focus of the study: _____

Questions I want to answer (add as many lines as needed):

_____

Sources I plan to use (check at least 5):

Books ___; Interviews ___; Experiments ___; Magazines___;
Encyclopedia___; Newspapers___; Museums___; Pictures, Films, Videos___;
Other Sources/ My Research___

Explain: _____

The finished product will be in the form of: _____

The learning skills I will use: _____

The study will be completed by (different dates may be given for various segments):

_____

The study will be reviewed by: _____

Evaluated by: _____

The evaluator will be looking for: _____

Student's Signature _____

Teacher's Signature _____

Sample checklist that might be used to evaluate a student's portfolio

Portfolio Assessment
Student's Name: _____
Class: _____
Date: _____

Attribute To Be Evaluated	Rating Scale				
	Very Good A	Good B	Average C	Poor D	Very Poor F
Originality					
Creativity					
Critical Thinking					
Research Skills					
Responsibility					
Perseverance					
Communication					

NOTE: can be modified to reflect class requirements, teacher preferences and rating scale.

Book response journal, comparison chart, and conferences

The **Book Response Journal** is a place for students to express their feelings about concepts and ideas discovered in the literature they read whether in a book, magazine, on the internet, or some other source of information. Students are encouraged to use these journals to comment on everything which they read. Teachers can use the journals as a way to ask questions, comment on the student's observations, and suggest additional reading material. Book response journals can and probably should be reviewed in student-teacher conferences.

Comparison Charts are a graphic way to organize ideas, events, characters, plot lines, and the like so that they can be compared and contrasted. They can be used by individual students and are a very effective tool for small groups to use in order to generate lively discussions.

The main purpose of a **Conference** is to collaborate, assess, and guide. They can be used for setting goals, coaching and mentoring, and evaluating the student's progress.

Demonstration, discussion, goal setting, and I learned statement

A Demonstration turns a concept into a concrete, observable experience using one or more of the five senses. It can be an audio-visual presentation, a piece of art or music, or a personal interpretation using drama or dance. It can be an experiment or an explanation of how something works.

A Discussion should be a safe forum for students to explore and explain ideas and concepts. They should be encouraged to speak, listen, and comment on and respond to their own and others' opinions, feelings, and reactions to a specific topic.

Goal Setting is an excellent way to help students learn to plan a project and experience success. It should be a collaborative effort with the teacher and encourage the student to reflect on his performance or lack thereof.

The purpose of an **I Learned Statement** is to encourage the student to express what he learned from a lecture, class discussion, homework assignment, or some other activity.

Graffiti wall, interview, and KWL technique

A **Graffiti Wall** is a designated area to brainstorm ideas, concepts, observations, questions, and conclusions about a topic. It can be used as an evolving record of the progress made by the group as they begin to understand the subject being researched and discussed. It can develop into a class dictionary and thesaurus used to enrich the students' vocabulary.

An **Interview** is a dialogue between the student and the teacher. Typically one or more questions are asked or problems posed in such a way as to determine the depth of understanding rather than to elicit specific answers.

A **KWL** is an effective way to assess how well the student grasped the concepts and can be used to judge the effectiveness of the teacher's lesson plan. The acronym stands for "Know," "Want," "Learned," and refers to what student knows and wants to know at the beginning of the lesson and what he has learned at the end of the lesson.

Learning logs, oral attitude survey, oral presentation, and problem-solving activity

A **Learning Log** is similar to a book response journal except that the student records his feelings about and responses to concepts and ideas covered in all of his classes. Keeping a log is a way to encourage critical thinking and improve writing skills.

Oral Attitude Surveys is a method to encourage students to share their own ideas, learn about the ideas of fellow students and think about topics from different perspectives. They can also evaluate their performance and rate the effectiveness of the discussion.

An Oral Presentation can be a speech, a dramatic recitation of a story or a poem, a video, or a debate that is evaluated using particular criteria.

A Problem-Solving Activity presents a question to the class. The group is expected to develop a method to find the answer and then solve the problem. Both the method and the solution are evaluated.

Rating scale that could be used for peer-assessments

Rating Scale
Student Being Rated: _____
Activity: _____
Student Doing The Rating: _____
Date: _____

Presents Argument Clearly		Demonstrates Background Knowledge	
☐	5 Very Logical	☐	5 Very Knowledgeable
☐	4 Logical	☐	4 Knowledgeable
☐	3 Average	☐	3 Average
☐	2 Not Very Logical	☐	2 Not All That Knowledgeable
☐	1 Totally Illogical	☐	1 Not Knowledgeable At All
Answers Relevant Questions		Organization	
☐	5 Very Relevant	☐	5 Very Organized
☐	4 Relevant	☐	4 Organized
☐	3 Average	☐	3 Average
☐	2 Some Relevance	☐	2 Not Always Organized
☐	1 No Relevance	☐	1 Not Organized At All

NOTE: can be modified to address different topics.

Data recording

There are three ways to record data about individual student performance. Each provides important information and lends itself to evaluating different aspects of student growth.

Anecdotal Records are observations of day-to-day activities, e.g., how the student interacts in a group, his ability to complete a hands-on assignment, his demeanor while taking tests, and his development of particular cognitive skills. All these offer opportunities for teacher comments.

The criteria on Observation Checklists vary depending on what the teacher wants to evaluate. They can be used to measure the growth of knowledge, a change in attitude, or the understanding of new skills. Checklists can also be used to evaluate written assignments, oral presentations, class participation, completion of individual and/or group work, or any activity that requires assessment.

Rating Scales are similar to observation checklists. The difference between the two is that checklists are used to determine the presence or absence of a skill, while rating scales measure the quality of the performance.

Anecdotal record

An anecdotal record is a written description of observed behavior. They are usually kept in an alphabetized book, binder, or folder and should be organized so it is easy to find notes concerning a particular student. There are computer programs available that make retrieving the data simple. To be effective, observations need to be made frequently and incidents need to be described completely and objectively; the teacher's analysis should be used as a guide for appropriate responses. Both successful situations and unsuccessful attempts need to be recorded in order to present an accurate picture of the student's progress.

The evaluation context is:
- Formative: recalling the incident may raise an alert that something that needs to be addressed.
- Summative: since observations are made over a period of time, they are an effective way to track student attitude, behavior, knowledge acquired, cognitive skills learned, etc.
- Diagnostic: consistent attention to performance may spotlight areas that need special attention.

Subject Under Discussion: _____

Students' Names: _____

Date and Time Period of Observations: _____

Demonstrated balance between talking and listening: _____

Demonstrated respect for others: _____

Actively participated in discussion: _____

Stated own opinion:

Acted as scribe:_____ Effectiveness: _____

Acted as reporter:_____ Effectiveness: _____

Acted as participant:_____ Effectiveness: _____

Acted as time-keeper:_____ Effectiveness: _____

  NOTE: form may be modified to fit the observer's particular requirements.

Observation checklist

Developing an observation checklist takes time. It can be helpful to write down all the skills, behaviors, attitudes, and processes required to acquire mastery of the subject and that are appropriate for the particular age group. The language should be simple and easy to understand, so that the checklists can be used during student and parent conferences. Items needed for the specific task or activity to be evaluated can be chosen from the master list. There should be no more than twelve items on a checklist: any more than that becomes difficult to track, especially when observing several students at the same time. Individual checklists can be developed for specific functions, e.g., participation in a class discussion, proficiency at using a microscope, the mechanics of preparing a term paper. Whatever the rating scale, it must be used consistently, applied fairly, and easy to use during the observation period.

An observation checklist is a list of specific skills, behaviors, attitudes, and processes that are relevant to a student's development and contribute to his ability to successfully complete learning activities. To be effective, these checklists need to be used frequently and be collected over a period of time. One or two observations can be misleading and will not provide an accurate measurement to reach a fair evaluation. Before a using a checklist, a teacher must decide upon its purpose, how and when it will be used, and what the criteria will be. During the observation period, all occurrences of each item shown on the list need to be recorded. It is helpful for later evaluation if the teacher has a quick reference shorthand system to describe each appearance, e.g., ! equals excellent, @ equals adequate, ? equals iffy, X equals inappropriate. After the session, notes should be added to clarify or elaborate the shorthand ratings.

Observation checklist that could be used to evaluate a class discussion

Observation Checklist

Subject Being Discussed: _____

Date: _____ Class: _____

Time Elapsed: _____

	Student Names		
Spoke Clearly			
Listened to Other Opinions			
Waited for turn			
Comment was Relevant			
Challenged a Comment			
Stated Reasons for Challenge			
Noticed a Discrepancy			
Stated a Relationship Between Ideas			
Offered a Conclusion			
Inclusive Behavior Shown			

NOTE: can be modified according to teacher requirements.

Rating scale

A rating scale is used to evaluate a student against a predetermined continuum. It is particularly useful for rating an oral presentation such as a speech, debate or stage performance, and for students to use as a self-assessment tool. To increase the scale's reliability, when developing the criteria to be evaluated, the activity needs to be broken into specific, manageable parts. Each criterion may need its own rating system. Scale points need to be created.

- Will the evaluation be based upon the one to five number scale with five being the highest, or
- Will the Very Good/Good/Average/Poor/Very Poor standard be used?
- Will another system be developed?

It is helpful for the teacher to decide at the beginning of the semester which units of study will be evaluated using this method and to develop the criteria and rating system ahead of time.

Oral presentations

Oral presentations offer a wealth of possibilities to evaluate student growth and development in several areas, including:

- Understanding of the subject,
- Planning and organizing abilities, and
- Communication skills.

This flexible assessment tool can be assigned to an individual student or as a group project. If given to a group, additional skills can be evaluated including response to other opinions, listening behaviors, active participation in discussions, and contributions to the work product. Teachers need to recognize that some students may have difficulty with or little or no experience conceptualizing, organizing, and delivering a presentation. To address these issues as well as any performance anxieties, it is necessary to establish a classroom atmosphere of acceptance so that students feel confident when giving a presentation. Allowing students some control over the choice of topic also helps alleviate some of the stress involved in standing up in front of the group.

Rating Scale For An Oral Presentation

Student's Name: _____

Date & Class Period:

	5	4	3	2	1
Voice is well modulated.					
Presentation is well paced.					
Pauses and emphases are appropriate.					
Can be heard easily by everyone.					
Material is: Organized					
Logical					
Interesting					
Good preparation is evident.					
Information used is on topic.					
Language is appropriate.					
Creativity in preparation and presentation.					
Audience is involved.					

Written assignments, presentations, performance assessments, and homework

Students are expected to engage in and complete various activities as a normal part of daily classroom participation. Teachers not only rate work products but they can and should use these activities to gauge progress in other goals such as social development, communication skills, and cognitive growth.

- Written Assignments: The ability to plan, organize, and produce a coherent, well-written essay, report, or term paper is just as important as the content of the finished product.
- Presentations: Whether planned or spontaneous, oral presentations need to be organized, logical, and engage the attention of the audience.
- Performance Assessment: Evaluating a student's participation and performance is important for helping him develop social and communicational skills.
- Homework: Homework requires independent study, planning skills, and the ability to prioritize. The student is expected to remember to do the work and turn it in by the required deadline.

Written assignments

Written assignments can take many forms, including essays, reports, term papers, short answers questions, journal and log entries, letters, articles, poetry, solutions to math puzzles, and research, to name a few. It is important that the teacher's expectations and the rating scale are explained with as much detail as possible, especially if students are unfamiliar with the process or are afraid of writing in general. The entire process should be reviewed: choosing a topic, planning, organizing, researching, outlining, writing a first draft, reviewing content, editing, writing a second draft, proofreading, asking someone to read the final draft, and meeting the deadline. Criteria need to be developed for each segment so that when the student and teacher meet for regular consultations during the process, there is a framework for discussion. If it is a group project, it is critical for the teacher to monitor the progress and make sure that every student is contributing to each phase of the process.

Oral assessments

Oral assessments are used for two reasons: when written assessments are not feasible, and to evaluate a student's mastery of such topics as verbal language proficiency, debating skills, and the ability to think and respond quickly. These types of assessments can be stressful and some students may have trouble responding and become tongue-tied; and therefore it is important to conduct the session in private or in an atmosphere of acceptance. As an interactive form of communication, the teacher needs to avoid filling in the blanks and providing body language clues that might influence the student's response. It is also important to avoid accentuating gender, race, or cultural differences in the content or delivery of the questions and/or tasks. The examination period should be long enough and the tasks required general enough in order to ensure that the student's knowledge and proficiency can be adequately presented and evaluated.

Performance test

A performance test is used to evaluate a particular skill that is one of the primary objectives of the class. Playing a musical instrument, using the backhand stroke in tennis, making a dress, doing a tune-up on a motor vehicle, and conducting a lab experiment are all skills that can be tested using this method. The teacher must ensure that the same criteria are used to evaluate each student and that every student has the same amount of time to demonstrate the skill. If it is an outdoor activity, climate conditions should be considered. Students need to be informed ahead of time on what they will be evaluated and when it will take place. In designing a performance task, teachers should be as specific as possible and consider the objective carefully. Students should be evaluated on both the process and the results. An observation checklist or rating scale is helpful in evaluating a performance test.

Performance assessments

Performance assessments are used to evaluate students' progress in specific tasks like demonstrating a skill, solving a complex problem with multiple parts, or participating in a general classroom discussion. The teacher is looking for what the student has learned and retained through what he does and not merely what he says. Information gathered through performance assessments is easy to communicate to students and parents because it describes observable, verifiable actions and offers concrete discussion points to use during conferences. There are four steps to successfully integrate performance assessments into a balanced, comprehensive view of student progress:
- Identify what is to be observed and assessed.
- Develop the criteria to be used.
- Decide which recording method to use between anecdotal records, an observation checklist, or a rating scale.
- Inform the students that they are being evaluated, on what they are being evaluated, and the criteria being used.

Homework

Homework should never be assigned as punishment or due to the teacher falling behind as a result of a poorly executed lesson plan or due to outside circumstances. It should be used if students are unable to complete a project during class, to gather information, to practice new skills, or to devise a solution to a complex problem based on a real life situation. Assigned tasks should be interesting and relevant to the students' daily experiences.

Guidelines for assigning homework:

- Provide clear, unambiguous, written instructions.
- Explain what is expected and how the results will be evaluated.
- Answer questions and address concerns.
- Make sure the due date is reasonable.
- Consider other academic requirements students may have.
- Be sure resource material is adequate and readily available.
- Collect the assignment on the date specified, grade it, and return it promptly.
- Be consistent with assessment protocol and provide thoughtful, helpful comments.

Writing quality tests and quizzes

Tests need to ask the right questions to accurately measure students' knowledge. There are several things to consider:

- Does each item represent an important idea or concept? If students understand the main objectives, their knowledge should be evident in their responses.
- Is each item an appropriate measure of the desired objective? Consider information presented and teaching strategies used.
- Are items presented in easily comprehensible language with clearly defined tasks? Students should not have to decode words or wonder what the item is asking them to do.
- Is the difficulty of the item appropriate? It should not be too difficult or too easy to complete.
- Is each item independent and free from overlap? Completing one item should not lead to completing additional items.
- Is the subject matter covered adequately?
- Is the test free of gender, class, and racial bias? Choose examples that are either familiar or unfamiliar to everyone.

Evaluating the effectiveness of a test

Teachers should have confidence that a test accurately measures students' knowledge: therefore it is important to monitor its effectiveness each time it is used. Before the test is given, all items should be reviewed to ensure that they still meet the criteria established for understanding the material and if one item does not meet the criteria, either rework it or remove it. If most students, including the better ones, miss the same question, perhaps it is too difficult or is not worded properly. If the item is salvageable, rework it, and if not, delete it. Asking for student feedback on one or two items is an effective way to determine if they are still appropriate or if they should be reworked or removed. Veteran teachers usually develop a "feel" for whether a test is an accurate reflection of what students know. If individual items or entire tests are reused, it is imperative to keep them in a secure place to minimize the possibility of cheating.

Sample checklist that could be used to evaluate a written assignment

Checklist for written assignment

Student Name: _____

Class: _____

Title of Paper: _____

	Yes	No	Comments
Understood objectives & requirements			
Met the timeline due dates			
Understood criteria for evaluation			
Actively participated in consultations			
Responded appropriately to suggestions			
Used reliable research sources			
Developed & followed a workable outline			
Used examples of prior knowledge			
Used good analytical & reasoning skills			
Developed good questions & answered them			
Worked in a methodical manner			
Used good grammar, sentence structure, spelling			

NOTE: May be modified to reflect teacher's particular requirements.

Checklist that can be used to evaluate how well a student understands the subject and expresses the concepts to the group

Assessment of Subject Understanding And Ability To Orally Present Concepts

Student Name: _____

Class: _____

Brief Description of Topic: _____

☐	Obviously read the material/watched the film/listened to the tape of background information.
☐	Able to identify main ideas and concepts.
☐	Information organized and presented logically.
☐	Showed evidence of prior knowledge and/or understanding of the topic.
☐	Creatively linked new data with prior knowledge.
☐	Defended position clearly and logically using good examples and solid reasoning.
☐	Accepted criticism from teacher and peers of reasoning used and position taken.
☐	Able to be heard by everyone.
☐	Spoke clearly with good cadence and used proper English.
☐	Keep audience interested and engaged.

NOTE: may be modified to meet teacher requirements.

Extended open-response items

Extended open-response items can be evaluated using either holistic scoring or analytic scoring; there is not much difference in reliability and effectiveness between the two methods. Holistic scoring measures a list of specific elements, e.g., clarity of the objective, choice of ideas explored, persuasiveness of the arguments, effectiveness of vocabulary, sentence structure, and organization of the essay. Each item is recognized and noted and the final grade is based upon the response as a whole.

Analytic scoring can evaluate the same elements but the difference is that each one is given a rating and the final grade is a sum of those rating values. For example: clarity earns twenty of twenty-five, choice of ideas earns eighteen of twenty, persuasiveness earns twenty-five of twenty-five, vocabulary and sentence structure earns fifteen of fifteen, and organization earns twelve of fifteen for a final grade of ninety. Analytic scoring evaluates with a little more detail than holistic scoring.

Using an extended open-response item is a very effective method to determine how well students understand the subject matter. This type of item measures students' ability to evaluate and synthesize information and how effectively they communicate using the written word. Depending upon how the item is worded, it allows students to describe and explain, compare and contrast, and develop and summarize the ideas and concepts learned. Since one item might be easier to answer than another, it is better to give all the students the same information to consider so that the evaluation is based upon the same premise. It is important that students understand beforehand the criteria that will be used to assess the response. Accurate facts and figures; a clear, concise writing style; and persuasive arguments might be the focus of the evaluation or perhaps rather the focus is creative expression, personal opinions, and/or conclusions and critical thinking.

Short-answer items

Short-answer items require a specific answer to a specific question. They can be a one or two word response, a brief definition, or a short paragraph. They are helpful when a teacher wants to know how well students have learned individual facts, figures, dates, definitions, etc. When using a completion or fill in the blank item, the answer should be placed at the end of the statement. This gives the student the opportunity to read all available information before having to answer. For example: Bright, bold, beautiful is an example of _____. The response (alliteration) is a one-word answer. If the answer requires more information, the instructions need to clearly state how much data is required. For example, "Give three important reasons the United States became involved in World War II." Multiple choice and true/false questions can be turned into short answer questions by requiring a brief explanation justifying the choice.

Matching item lists

Matching items are used to test recall of specific facts. This is a quick, effective method to determine how well students have integrated information and made associations. The first step is to group homogeneous facts together and then develop parallel lists of premises and responses. The information needs to be closely related; if it is not, common sense instead of knowledge of the subject will dictate the matches. List items randomly to avoid providing clues as to what premise matches which response, e.g., alphabetically by first word or by length of answer. Keep lists manageable as too many items can be confusing. The entire question needs to be on the same page; dividing it between two wastes time and changes the dynamics. Having the students group related facts and develop premises and responses as a class exercise is a good method to review the material. It also provides data to use on a future test.

Multiple choice item lists

A multiple choice item has a direct question or a complete statement called the stem, which is followed by several possible answers of which usually only one is correct (multiple responses can be requested). These items are designed to test recall and recognition of facts as well as the ability to make associations. The stem needs to be stated in such as a way as to require a specific answer. The language needs to be simple, short, and concise but must include enough data and state the information clearly enough that there is no confusion. Avoid using clues that might indicate the correct answer and be wary of using "all of the above" and "none of the above" as possible responses. These too cause confusion. Ensure that the stem of one item does not include the answer to another. Asking for the correct or incorrect answer is common. Asking for the best answer requires using critical thinking skills.

True/false item lists

Depending upon how they are worded, true/false items can be used to test content knowledge, recall of facts, ability to define and/or use an idea or concept, and to evaluate information. The most efficient way to develop true/false items is to review textbooks and other resource material and make a list of ideas, concepts, facts, and miscellaneous data. It is important to construct the statement using clear, concise language that is grammatically correct and unambiguous. In order to avoid confusion, use only one idea, concept, or fact in each question. Make the statement positive rather than negative. If using a negative statement, make sure its negativity is clear. The idea is to challenge, not confuse students. Use more false items than true ones because, statistically, guessers tend to check true more often than false. Try to include some plausible false answers but avoid trick questions.

Preparing tests

It is a good idea to use several types of questions when preparing tests. This will prevent the students from getting bored, expose them to a variety of testing formats, and encourage them to recall and respond to information in different ways. Matching and true/false questions are an excellent way to quickly assess how well students remember specific facts, as well as their ability to memorize data. Multiple choice and short-answer questions require a little deeper knowledge of the subject and better reasoning and thinking skills. These four testing options are reasonably quick and easy to grade. Open-response questions can be used to evaluate in depth content knowledge, the use of critical thinking skills, and the ability to communicate thoughts and ideas through the written word. This option requires more time, effort, and concentration to evaluate fairly, and is a more effective tool in some situations and courses than it is in others.

Effective time management ideas

Effective time management is crucial for every teacher. Accurate, fair assessment of students' academic and social progress is equally important. It is critical to develop ways to accomplish both efficiently. Organization is a key ingredient in the equation; time spent searching for things is time wasted. Collaborating with colleagues to develop assessment tools; sharing instructional methods, testing techniques, and formats that work; and establishing standards and priorities for evaluations take time in the beginning but ultimately save time. Teachers who expect perfection from themselves and/or their students are striving to reach an unrealistic goal. Using evaluation tools with appropriate frequency, assessing their value at regular intervals, constructing and saving good testing items, and using standard formats when possible are all ways to use time efficiently. Preparing lessons, organizing record keeping and evaluating the effectiveness of each on a regular basis will help develop a sensible, workable use of limited time resources.

Content Area Instruction

Problems students may have learning English grammar, spelling and vocabulary

The English language has one of the largest vocabularies of any language currently in use. English has adopted, adapted and integrated words, phrases and expressions from many other languages. English uses more idiomatic words and phrases than most other languages and these idioms can be specific to a particular region of the country or a segment of the population. The same word can be used in multiple ways and have different meanings (i.e. to "spell" a word or come sit a "spell") or two words can sound alike but be spelled differently and have different meanings (i.e. wood and would). English often uses articles, such as "the," "a" and "an" while other languages may lack articles altogether or use their versions sparingly. There isn't just one rule to make a positive word into its negative counterpart. For example: **un**able, **in**appropriate, **dis**honest, **a**moral. All of these differences can make learning the English language a challenge.

Transaction with the text

Transaction with the text means the reader has a dialogue with the printed material. He is actively engaged in the process; he is participating in the exchange of ideas and information. At the secondary level, there are two types of transactions: the efferent stance and the aesthetic stance.

In the efferent stance, the reader is gathering information and uses his background knowledge objectively.

The aesthetic stance involves a personal response. The words bring back memories, recall emotions, and retrieve experiences stored in the reader's background knowledge. Proficient readers are able to use the aesthetic stance while gathering information. For example factual data about London might jog memories of a family vacation in the city. Students will improve their reading skills if the material is responsive to their culture and recognizes their differences. The goal is for all students to be able to effectively transact with the text.

Language, vocabulary, pronunciation and grammar

The American Heritage College Dictionary defines language as "voice sounds and written symbols representing these sounds, in combinations and patterns, used to express and communicate thoughts and feelings." Vocabulary is "all the words of a language." Pronunciation is a "way of speaking a word, especially a way that is accepted and generally understood." Grammar is the "rules of a language viewed as a mechanism for generating all sentences possible in that language."

Vocabulary (a set of words), pronunciation (how the words are spoken) and grammar (rules governing how to use the words) are all vital elements in learning, understanding and properly using a language. If one or more elements are not learned, learned inadequately, ignored or misused, communication is impaired. The depth of a person's vocabulary and his ability to speak and write effectively is often used as a measurement of his intelligence and frequently reflects the level and quality of his education.

Components of language

There are four main components of all languages: reading, writing, speaking and hearing. The following definitions are from The American Heritage College Dictionary.

Reading is "the act or activity of rendering text aloud." To Read is "the ability to examine and grasp the meaning of written and printed material in a given language."

Writing is "meaningful letters or characters that constitute readable material." To Write is "to form letters, words or symbols on a surface such as paper with an instrument such as a pen." (People also use typewriters and computer keyboards.)

Speaking is being "capable of speech involving talking, expressing or telling." To Speak is "to convey thoughts, opinions or emotions orally."

Hearing is "the sense by which sound is perceived." To Hear is "to be capable of perceiving sound by the ear."

Good reading skills as it relates to language

Reading is the process of understanding written information and ideas. Before the industrial revolution in the late nineteenth and early twentieth centuries, only a small percentage of the population was literate. The skill wasn't deemed necessary for most people. Preventing certain segments of the community from learning to read was also an effective way to keep them from fully participating in society.

There are several reasons for reading: memorizing, learning and comprehension, skimming, scanning and proofreading. All have their uses. Proofreading detects errors in grammar and content. Skimming and scanning are used to process large quantities of information quickly when just surface comprehension is needed. Memorizing remembers and stores information for later retrieval. Understanding and comprehension are the main reasons most people read. Some read because they are required to for school or work, some to expand their general knowledge, and some read simply because they enjoy it.

Reading tests

Reading ability can be tested in several ways depending upon what skill is being measured. Some reading tests use more than one of the components shown below. Different tests or variations of the same test are used to measure children, adolescents and adults. These are the most common reading tests used to determine various reading skills:
- **Sight Word Reading**: the person is given words of increasing difficulty. Longer, more complicated, less common words are used until he can't pronounce and doesn't understand them.
- **Non-Word Reading**: the person is given nonsense words to read out loud until they become too difficult or complex to pronounce.
- **Reading Comprehension**: the person reads a passage (silently or out loud) and answers questions about the content.
- **Reading Speed**: how fast a person reads the words.
- **Reading Accuracy**: the person's ability to read words correctly.

Writing as it relates to language

Writing is the method used to preserve information using letters and words as opposed to drawings, paintings, verbal recordings and moving pictures. The act of writing is distinctly human. No other animal has the dexterity to form the letters or the intelligence to put them into meaningful order. Writing as a noun is the written word; writing as a verb is the act of forming the letters in the word.

Writing is composed of penmanship, spelling and talent. Even in a world of computers, handwriting (penmanship) should be legible. A person should be able to form the letters by hand so they are clearly distinguishable. Reading comprehension

- *61* -

is dependent on recognizing the words in the text; a poor speller limits his ability to recognize and understand words. Talent is the ability to express thoughts and feelings via the written word. Spelling and grammar can be taught; talent is inborn; it can only be nurtured.

Speaking and hearing

Speaking is used to convey thoughts, ideas and emotions. It helps develop bonds between individuals and enhances social interaction within and between groups. It is important to the preservation of a culture because it is used to explain, educate and pass on tribal traditions. In early human history, before the written word was created, speaking was the only method available to ensure that civilizations continued from one generation to the next. Communication is a bidirectional process that involves a speaker and an active listener, and these two parts must both work for thoughts, ideas and emotions to be conveyed; if no one hears what someone is saying, there is no possibility of communication. After the written word came into use and books became available, speaking and hearing were still important because reading for the common man has only been encouraged for about the past one hundred and fifty years.

Speech development if a child has a hearing problem

The ability to speak develops in the first few years. If a child has a hearing problem, speech will be delayed or disabled. He will have trouble communicating and difficulty learning the skills necessary to function independently. (If a child is profoundly hearing impaired [deaf], sign language and Braille are available to enable communication.) The earlier a hearing problem is recognized, diagnosed and treated, the better the chance to avoid life-long problems with speech and hearing issues. Hearing impairment causes difficulty with learning to read which leads to difficulty with the mechanics of writing (penmanship) and the ability to write (express thoughts, ideas and emotions in written words). A person who hears and knows how to speak will not lose his ability to read if he develops a hearing problem later in life. However, if a person never hears well enough to learn to speak, he will rarely be able to read proficiently.

English Language Learners instructional methods using the native language of the student

There are four English Language Learner (ELL) programs that use the student's native language while he is learning English.
- Transitional Bilingual programs use the native language in core academic subjects. The goal, however, is to phase into English–only courses as quickly as possible.
- Developmental Bilingual programs use the native language in core academic subjects throughout elementary school. Sometimes the program extends into

middle and high school even after the student has been classified proficient in English.

- In Two-Way Immersion programs, the students are from similar backgrounds with about half of the class speaking the native language and the other half speaking both. Instruction is about evenly split between English and the native language.
- Newcomer programs are usually reserved for recent U.S. arrivals. Instruction is in the native language and students are also helped to acclimate to their new environment.

English Language Learners instructional methods using the native language as support

The four English Language Learner (ELL) programs (transitional bilingual, developmental bilingual, two-way immersion and newcomer) all use the students' native language as part of the instructional design and plan lessons allowing for a slower pace. There is one ELL method in which instead of switching back and forth between the native language and English, it instead uses the native language in a support role only. Students learning English are placed in mainstream classrooms and instruction is entirely in English with a bilingual paraprofessional available to provide assistance. These paraprofessionals translate vocabulary, explain lessons presented in English and clarify confusing assignments. This method is partially based on the theory that interacting on a daily basis with teachers and students whose native language is English also helps the ELL student learn English more quickly and makes acclimating to the new culture easier.

Methods used to teach English as a Second Language

The three methods most commonly used to teach English as a Second Language (ESL) are grammar-based, communication-based and content-based. Grammar-based ESL teaches students the rules of English including structure, function and vocabulary. Emphasis is on the why and how of the language. Communication-based ESL teaches students how to use English in every day, realistic situations. This approach emphasizes practical conversational usage. Content-based ESL teaches students grammar and vocabulary and uses written assignments in order to practice these skills. This approach includes using English as the main method of classroom communication between the teacher and the student and amongst students. This method emphasizes an integrated approach to learning English.

Continuum of learning theory

The Continuum of Learning theory outlines predictable steps when learning a new language.
- The Silent/Receptive or Preproduction stage can last from a few hours to six months. Students usually don't say much and communicate by using pictures and pointing.
- In the Early Production stage, students use one- and two-word phrases. They indicate understanding with yes or no and who/what/where questions. This stage can last six months.
- The Speech Emergence stage may last a year. Students use short sentences and begin to ask simple questions. Grammatical errors may make communication challenging.
- In the Intermediate Language Proficiency stage students begin to make complex statements, share thoughts and opinions and speak more often. This may last a year or more.
- The Advanced Learning Proficiency stage lasts five to seven years. Students have acquired a substantial vocabulary and are capable of participating fully in classroom activities and discussions.

Interpersonal communication skills

Basic interpersonal communication skills encompass two different and distinct styles of communication:
- In context-embedded communication, various visual and vocal props are available to help the student understand that which is being said, including pictures and other objects to graphically explain and communicate demonstratively. The speaker's gestures and tone of voice help the listener understand the words being used. Conversations with speakers who use hand gestures and stories with pictures and props help the learners understand more quickly and easily.
- Context-reduced communication does not have visual clues and cues and therefore the learner must rely on his competency and fluency in the language. Phone conversations, for example, do not allow the listener to see the speaker and thus hand gestures and facial expressions and other visual aides are missing. Reading a note without pictorial guides may make it difficult for the student to understand the written words.

Cognitive demands made when communicating

Depending upon with whom the conversation is had, where it is occurring and the complexity of the subject, different cognitive abilities are required of the speaker and the listener. When a student is in a relaxed, informal setting such as on the playground or in the lunchroom, the conversation between listener and speaker does not require a great deal of abstract or critical thinking. When a teacher asks a simple question requiring a yes or no answer, it is usually not threatening or stress producing. This is a cognitively undemanding communication. However, when the student is required to hear, analyze and respond quickly to abstract or complex ideas and concepts, he suddenly finds himself in a cognitively demanding communication situation. These encounters can happen during classroom discussions, when meeting new people and in unfamiliar surroundings and can pose significant challenges for learners.

Key principles of language acquisition for English Language Learners

There are four key concepts teachers in mainstream classrooms can use to help English Language Learners (ELL) acquire proficiency in both written and spoken English.

- **Increase Comprehensibility** of the content of lesson plans and activities. Use pictures, props, gestures and voice variations to explain and demonstrate the subject. Build on the language concepts the student already has.
- **Encourage Interaction** by asking questions and assigning group activities. This provides the student with many opportunities to practice that which he knows and increase his confidence so that he is able to learn more effectively.
- **Increase Thinking and Study Skills** by asking thought-provoking questions and assigning complex topics for research and writing projects. Establish and expect the same high standards from every student.
- **Use The Native Language** to increase understanding and comprehension. Translating questions and assignments into the student's native language clarifies instructions and helps him understand that which is expected.

Strategies and approaches for teaching English language learners

In general, researchers have been unable to prove conclusively and empirically that any particular strategy for teaching English as a second language is effective in increasing retention, proficiency and fluency. The methods used to collect data are inconsistent and oftentimes studies don't compare information from both control groups and non-control groups. When comparisons are made, they sometimes do not consider the ages and stages of the groups studied. The evidence that does exist comes from anecdotal observations, surveys and case studies. What has been determined is that most successful classroom methods incorporate several approaches and the effectiveness of each depends upon the age of the students and the degree of language proficiency already attained.

Strategies and approaches should be viewed as starting points for teachers in mainstream classrooms to review and consider. Choices should be made based on the students involved and the environment in which the instruction takes place.

Total Physical Response and Cooperative Learning strategies

Developed by James J. Asher in the 1960s, **Total Physical Response (TPR)** uses physical activity to reinforce the words and phrases being taught. Depending upon the age and level of language proficiency, students are given a series of simple to complex commands and/or instructions. They are expected to respond appropriately. TPR is a tool that is effective when incorporated with other methods.

In 1995 Robert E. Slavin demonstrated that **Cooperative Learning** is an effective tool no matter what the students' age or level of proficiency. Pairing English language learners (ELL) and students whose native language is English in small group activities is very effective for a number of reasons. As long as a well-structured task is assigned, students learn to work together as a team and the ELL students get to practice conversational skills while watching others' study habits. It also allows English-speaking students to interact with ELL students in a non-threatening setting.

Language Experience Approach and using Dialogue Journals

In the **Language Experience Approach** (also called Dictated Stories), either the teacher or a fellow student transcribes the language learner's words as he verbally relates a personal experience in his native language. The written English version is then used as a reading lesson when the language learner reads the translated story to the class. This tool shows the student how his native language is encoded into English and helps build word recognition while improving fluency. It also educates the other students about a different culture.

Dialogue Journals (also called Interactive Journals) help the student learn how to write English. He keeps a journal of his thoughts, feelings and impressions. The purpose is not to evaluate the content but to offer a non-threatening avenue for the teacher to answer questions and correct grammar and spelling errors. It also provides a method for the student to privately communicate with someone who is proficient in English.

Academic Language Scaffolding and Native Language Support

Academic Language Scaffolding is a gradual step-by-step process that builds on the English language learner's knowledge and confidence as he learns to complete tasks independently and communicate more fluently. A teacher using this approach needs to consistently speak using proper English during lectures and while giving instructions, use expressive gestures and informative demonstrations and assign hands-on activities and projects that reinforce the lessons.

No matter what other methods are used, **Native Language Support** should be available to the English Language Learner. Even when the teacher doesn't speak his language and the student is in an English-only classroom, he should have access to someone who speaks his native language. It provides him with the opportunity to have instructions and assignments clarified and encourages active participation in classroom activities. Decorating the classroom with posters and other objects from his native country shows respect for his language and culture.

Accessing Prior Knowledge and Cultural Studies

No matter what the age or level of English proficiency, students come to school with knowledge and experience. Building on and **Accessing Prior Knowledge** encourages them to explore new ideas and learn new concepts. A teacher who asks the student what he already knows about the subject and then lets him decide that which he wants to discover creates a positive environment in which to learn. If a student is interested in a topic, he is usually more excited about and engaged in learning more.

The effectiveness of including the student's native culture in the classroom is well documented. English language learners assigned a **Culture Study** project are encouraged to share information about their cultural history. The assignment requires research, writing, creating visual aids and giving an oral presentation. It may also include interviewing parents, siblings, grandparents and friends.

Encouraging cross-cultural understanding

Society is diverse and schools reflect that diversity. Teachers play an important role in helping students understand and learn to appreciate various cultures. Asking English language learners to tell a story, popular in their home country, in their native language and then translating it into English builds confidence. Sharing a favorite object from their homeland and explaining what it is, how it is made and for what purpose it is used encourages an appreciation for other cultures.

An effective strategy to address issues that arise between students with different cultural heritages is called misunderstandings. A student shares an incident that caused a problem. Words said, body language used, social customs encountered and stereotypes perceived are just some of the things that may be involved. As students discuss the situation, ask questions and get answers, they gain insight into the complexities of cultural differences and the importance of accurate cultural awareness and understanding.

Potential problems that may be encountered while learning the English language

Many people study the English language because it is spoken in several countries; in some situations, it is the accepted and preferred language in which international business is conducted. Because there is no cross-cultural standard for English as there is for other languages (i.e. French and Spanish), there are very real differences in pronunciation, vocabulary and grammar depending upon the region and within the same area because of social groups and educational levels.

The degree of difficulty learning English can sometimes be attributed to how greatly the student's native language differs from English. For example, a person who speaks French or Spanish might find it easier to learn English than would a person who speaks Chinese or Russian. No matter what the native language or the language being studied, students may have problems with pronunciation, grammar, spelling and vocabulary. Some may learn to speak the new language with some proficiency but have difficulties writing it.

Pronunciation problems

Variations in consonant and vowel sounds can cause problems and make the pronunciation of English language learners sound stilted, monotone and flat. For example, the "th" combination is relatively rare in other languages so it is hard for some students to pronounce. American English has sixteen different combinations of vowels with sometimes only slight variations in the sound of the spoken word. Many languages have very few vowel sounds which means students can have problems hearing, and consequently, pronouncing these sounds. English allows for clusters of consonants before a vowel if needed, while several other languages do not. Therefore students may try to insert a vowel where there is none.

Stressed and unstressed vowels can be very confusing for English language learners. Native English speakers can determine the pronunciation by the word's placement in a sentence; learners sometimes can't distinguish the slight variations. For example: able, enable, unable.

Differences between written and spoken English

Spoken English sounds different depending upon the country of origin, geographic location within the country, the particular idioms used in a region, the educational level of the speaker and his ethnic and cultural heritage. Dialects, accents and slang all influence how a person speaks. Two English speakers from different countries may have difficulty understanding one another because of these variations. A third party listening to the conversation might think they were speaking totally different languages. Written English, on the other hand, is based on a defined set of rules (grammar) so that a person reading a document written in formal English would not be able to determine from which country or region the writer originates. The only indication might be the way a word is spelled (e.g., colour instead of color) or the context in which it is used (lift instead of elevator). These variations, however, would not prevent the reader from understanding the material.

Improving the experience of the English Language Learner

A teacher who has English Language Learners in his mainstream classroom, no matter what the subject area may be, can do many things to help ELL students learn and improve their pronunciation and comprehension. Enunciating clearly, speaking in a normal volume and at a normal pace, avoiding idioms and slang, using appropriate gestures, and pointing to pictures and objects are all beneficial. Because many language learners have trouble reading and understanding cursive, it helps to print information and instructions clearly and legibly on the board and also when correcting papers. Making sure objectives and activities are clearly explained and questions are answered before beginning the lesson helps to prevent misunderstandings. Repeating, reviewing, rephrasing, and summarizing frequently and using short sentences helps students organize and integrate data. Praising students when praise is merited is always effective unless the student's cultural heritage considers individual attention inappropriate, in which case a private word is a better approach. Good classroom management and a predictable routine contribute to everyone's success.

Phonics

Phonics is an analytical approach to reading. Students take words apart to study individual letters and how they come together to make sounds. These letter-sound combinations form syllables. When syllables are combined, they become a word. Learning to decode or "sound-out" letter combinations enables students to visually recognize words they already hear and speak in every day conversation. It gives students the tools to sound-out unfamiliar words they discover as they explore new subjects and helps expand students' vocabulary by giving them a way to pronounce new words. Phonics helps students learn to spell because most words are spelled like they sound. Consonants have a speech-sound relationship, but the few exceptions need to be memorized. Vowels, however, don't always have a predictable speech-sound relationship. They are influenced by the surrounding letters, the stress placed on the particular syllable and the sentence in which the word is found.

What happens in an actual classroom setting when students are learning to read

There are positives and negatives to both phonics and the whole language approach to reading. Phonics provides a dependable way for students to "sound out" unfamiliar words, but often requires monotonous repetition, memorization, and completing worksheets, which can often be boring. The whole language approach emphasizes learning the meaning of words in context but does not provide students with a method to decipher new words. Teachers who teach reading or assign oral presentations usually eventually use a combination of both approaches even if they are not aware of it. They help stumbling students disassemble words and sound out each syllable (phonics) because sometimes that is the only way the student can figure out how to pronounce the word. They ask students probing, open-ended questions about the context in which the new word appears in order to help them figure out what the word means (whole language).

Print exposure

Print exposure is the amount of time a person spends reading. He can read fiction and non-fiction books, school and local newspapers, entertainment and news magazines, and professional and scientific journals; reading anything has lasting cognitive consequences. Research has shown that reading, not oral language, is the most effective way to increase one's vocabulary at any age. The conversations between adults contain fewer advanced words than a book for preschoolers. Television scripts and radio commentary is the same, even programs devoted to hard news coverage.

This is because oral language is very repetitive and people seldom venture out of their verbal comfort zone. Therefore, in order for a student to improve and increase his vocabulary, he needs to read from a wide variety of written sources. Frequent exposure to printed words helps students gain confidence in their speaking ability more quickly and easily than those who do not spend time reading.

Guided oral reading strategy

Guided oral reading is an instructional strategy used to improve verbal reading skills. Its main function is to improve fluency. This approach can be used with students of any age and grade. This exercise can be used at home, in the classroom with the whole group or in pairs (i.e., a fluent reader with a struggling student); the process is the same each way:
- A parent, teacher, or peer reads a passage aloud at about eighty (80) to one hundred (100) words per minute. The material needs to be at the student's level of comprehension.
- The student reads the text silently several times.
- The student reads the passage aloud. The parent, teacher, or peer offers encouragement and constructive feedback. It usually takes four times before the student is able to read the text without errors.

Helping ESL and ELL students in a mainstream classroom

English as a Second Language (ESL) and English Language Learners (ELL) pose unique challenges in a language arts classroom. Several activities enable them to learn conversational English more quickly which will help their ability to master grammar and syntax, understand literature, improve writing skills, and accelerate their acquisition of vocabulary:
- Pair an ESL/ELL with a native English speaker who explains an idiom, colloquialism, or slang term in simple language.
- Let ESL/ELL use a translation dictionary. It will ease the frustration of trying to determine the correct English word.
- Use lots of visual cues: pictures, illustrations, charts, etc.

- Emphasize key words with flashcards. Have students alternate between recognizing the word, the definition, and the picture.
- Have ESL/ELL students read the newspaper and/or watch the news on television and then summarize the information in a few sentences before presenting it to the class.

Negative influences on learning second or additional languages

The traditional method of teaching and learning new languages, often called the "Grammar Translation Method," has been associated through research findings with a lack of motivation and poorer results in learning new languages. These results are attributed to the inherently boring quality of the method. Methods of rote memorization, drilling, and practicing "Basic Dialogue Sentences," historically used in schools often are found similarly dull and uninspiring. Educators have found that more innovative, engaging, active, and interactive teaching and learning methods can motivate students more to learn new languages, enjoy learning more, and result in better learning. Another barrier exists with language disorders. For example, the brain disorder of aphasia interferes with a person's ability to understand spoken language (Wernicke's aphasia) or to express oneself in speech (Broca's aphasia) through finding words and constructing grammatical utterances. An additional negative factor is the "affective filter," which consists of aversive feelings such as discomfort, stress, self-consciousness, and/or lack of motivation associated with L2 learning, most common in adults and older teenagers.

Applying the principles of behaviorist theory regarding language learning

In order to teach ESL, a teacher likely would introduce lessons in English language and academic content subjects in small, manageable portions following the behaviorist principle of presenting new material in small amounts. This practice facilitates more precise shaping of new learned behaviors and enables ESL students to learn more easily. The educator would demonstrate spoken and written English in order to provide a model for students to imitate, another behaviorist principle. The teacher would be sure to reward correct student responses following the behaviorist principle of positive reinforcement, thereby increasing the students' likelihood of repeating these responses. Behaviorism finds that only outwardly observable and measurable behaviors can be changed and thus disregards internal states, which it cannot observe, measure, or change. As a result, the teacher would use tests, quizzes, in-class and homework assignments, etc. and score these assessments quantitatively in order to measure correct and incorrect responses. Increases in the former and decreases in the latter would indicate learning, which behaviorism defines as observable, measurable changes in behavior over time.

Approaches of ESL teachers that would reflect Chomsky's theory of language acquisition

According to Chomsky, learning language is not something that children actually do, but is a natural process occurring universally in children as they develop. Chomsky has stated that we live in a biological world; the body—including the brain, and the "language organ" he believes our brains inherently possess—physically matures over time according to predetermined patterns. Chomsky proposed that we are born with a Language Acquisition Device (LAD) in our brains, thereby facilitating language development. He allowed that children need proper nutrition and environmental stimulation in order to nurture the natural language development enabled by the LAD. Therefore, ESL teachers would want to ensure their students receive optimal physical nourishment and stimulus-rich environments, under the teacher's influence at school and at home inasmuch as this is possible. Because Chomsky that found all humans share Universal Grammar (UG) regardless of individual languages, teachers of ESL students would emphasize basic commonalities between students' L1s and English in order to help them relate the two languages. Differences could be addressed through correcting English errors over time as students' English proficiency progresses.

Albert Bandura's Social Learning Theory

Bandura's Social Learning Theory has been viewed as building a bridge between behaviorist theories such as Skinner's and cognitive theories such as Piaget's because Bandura's theory explains human behavior through mutual interactions among environmental, behavioral, and cognitive factors. Like Bruner, Bandura emphasizes the role of social influences in learning. While behaviorists believe that the environment produces changes in behavior, Bandura believed in addition to this that behavior also produces changes in the environment. Because interactions are always two-way in Bandura's view, he called this Reciprocal Determinism. While Bandura studied social phenomena such as adolescent aggression more than language development, his theory can be applied usefully to ESL teaching, especially in regard to modeling, imitation, and observational/vicarious learning. Conditions Bandura found required for modeling are: Attention, Retention, Reproduction, and Motivation. Imitating models is motivated not only by past events (as in behaviorism), but also by promised/anticipated rewards (internal expectations vs. behaviorism's external stimuli), and vicariously, i.e. observing another student receiving rewards for a behavior and imitating that modeled behavior to procure similar rewards.

Bruner's Interactionist theory emphasizes the social context of children's language learning. He found the interactions between children and their parents/caregivers and others the most important element in children's cognitive and language development. Teachers applying Bruner's principles would provide plenty of modeling of spoken and written English language for ESL students to imitate. While modeling to enable imitation is similar to applying behaviorist principles, behaviorism focuses only on environmental stimuli that shape behavior including language use, whereas Bruner's theory emphasizes the social environment and the ways that parent-child interactions promote language learning. Teachers should provide temporary support, which Bruner termed scaffolding, to ESL students, gradually withdrawing it as they gain more linguistic and academic proficiency in English. As one of the founders of constructivist theory, Bruner believed (as did Piaget) that we construct our own realities through forming new ideas based on the knowledge we have accumulated. Teachers can reflect this principle by offering ESL students opportunities/assignments involving active, direct participation in learning activities.

Applying the principles of Piaget's theory of cognitive development

Piaget maintained that children's intellectual development progresses in distinct stages, with each succeeding stage adding new, more advanced cognitive abilities. Furthermore, children can learn only in ways consistent with their current stage of cognitive development. Therefore, teachers should not expect the youngest ESL students to be able to perform mental operations yet or try to get them to understand logic. Piaget found young children are egocentric and cannot adopt another's perspective, so presenting lessons students can relate to from their own perspectives uses this natural egocentrism to facilitate learning. (Witness the many children's books using "I/me/my" and other first-person references in their titles and approaches.)   Public school curricula typically introduce arithmetic to elementary-school children at the ages of Piaget's Concrete Operations stage, when they first can perform and reverse mental operations with concrete objects. Teachers should not present entirely abstract concepts until students are beginning Formal Operations, usually in the preteen years. Teachers also should encourage ESL students' active experimentation and hands-on learning, as Piaget advocated.

Promoting empathy for ESL students and identify effective and ineffective teaching practices

Educators recommend that ESL teachers enroll in a foreign language course themselves, in order to become acquainted/reacquainted with how it feels to grapple with learning a non-native speech system. They also advise repeating this experience every few years, because even teachers who have already learned another language tend to forget how they felt as beginners. This exercise promotes teachers' patience and understanding with non-native students trying to learn English. To identify which of their teaching practices were most and least effective, teachers can keep a private teaching journal. What initially may seem like extra work and time spent becomes an invaluable, time-saving resource for future instruction: if teachers write down exactly what they did in a class and how students responded, they then can use these records to inform and improve each new day's lesson by not repeating previous unsuccessful practices and by practicing more of the methods and strategies that brought the most success for students.

Giving ESL lessons more structure to provide students with more cohesive instruction

Organizing what is taught and learned in ESL classes gives LEP students more structure, easing some of the bewilderment and challenges of learning English as a second language. Teachers can organize their lessons according to specific topics, which they can allow the students to select. This organization has the benefit of ensuring that a topic is interesting to the students, and it affords more cohesive learning than simply teaching a number of unrelated linguistic exercises. It allows teachers to adjust for the variety of learning and proficiency levels they find among students and for the disparity of levels some individual students present among the various domains of English-language and academic content performance. Organizing each lesson by limiting it to an individual topic—which can range from world peace to grocery shopping or anything in between—also allows the teacher to ensure that s/he provides each student with enough assistance focusing on the individual English-language skills they need to develop, such as pronunciation, spelling, reading, writing, spoken fluency, academic content vocabulary, and etc.

Studying in class the spoken English native speakers use in real everyday life

Some teachers have their ESL students carry small voice recorders with them as they go through everyday life, e.g. in stores, restaurants, at sporting events, at parties, and at workplaces where applicable. The students bring their recordings of real English conversations into class, where they can examine and study them. This exercise provides a more realistic and usable understanding of real spoken English, including common idioms, colloquialisms, slang, figures of speech, and social and cultural conventions than textbooks and academic exercises offer. Teachers also have their ESL students bring in forms used when dealing with government agencies, and for some high school students, from their respective workplaces. This strategy affords dual benefits of helping students work with the forms and familiarizing them with linguistic conventions used in such paperwork. Additionally, teachers can use the language samples their students obtain to develop role-play exercises in which the students can participate in order to give the students practice with social and business situations they will encounter at parties, meetings, restaurants, banks, stores, jobs, etc.

Practicing good teaching methods and saving time and effort

Educators find that instead of using many textbooks, worksheets, etc., wearing out the copy machine and themselves, teachers can expand thoroughly on each single material. Rather than assigning many stories to read with only one accompanying activity apiece, teachers can have students read one story, discuss the story in class, discuss the story among themselves, write about the story, write about what others have said/written about the story, read what other students have written about the story, get listening practice through dictation of the story; etc. An additional benefit of this thorough treatment is that repetition is crucial to second-language learning.

- 74 -

Another way that teachers of ESL students can save time while also pursuing a topic or material in more depth involves minimizing photocopying and/or making multiple printouts. For example, rather than copying 10 different exercises from a printed resource, they can copy one exercise and then come up with 10 different activities their students can do with it. In-class dictation also eliminates copying and provides listening and writing practice.

Guidelines teachers of ESL students should follow relative to informing students of teacher expectations and to teachers being prepared for classes

When teachers begin a class with ESL students, they should inform students of clear expectations related to class attendance, being on time, completing and turning in homework, classroom behavior, etc. Such disclosures will avert many future problems and misunderstandings. Teachers always should be prepared for classes by having made a lesson plan. Even very experienced teachers who could improvise likely have some kind of lesson plan. In addition, teachers should have backup plans. Progress in ESL classes can be unpredictable, varying from day to day in students' working speeds. Many ESL teachers keep short-term activity files handy, containing such learning activity resources as word games, riddles, collections of short articles on topics interesting to their students, and versions of these adapted with the vocabulary the class is currently learning. These activities can give ESL students variety or a break from the usual routines, additional activities when they complete lesson material more quickly, and/or reinforcement of the other activities and language of that day's lesson/class.

3x5 index cards can be an invaluable resource for ESL teachers

Some ESL teachers have remarked that they could teach English to ESL students easily using only 3x5 index cards and pens or markers. Educators find virtually unlimited language activities that can be done using index cards. For example, teachers can make flashcards using the fronts and backs of index cards. They can write individual words on cards for students to use in playing matching games—matching synonyms, antonyms, word categories, verb tenses, singular/plural nouns, concepts, etc. They can create text containing gaps in meaning and/or structure, write words on cards, and have students select the appropriate cards to fill in the missing information. They can use cards with individual words written on them to give ESL students practice in constructing sentences with the correct word order. They can have students play "Concentration"/memory games by identifying matching cards within grouped cards. Students can work in pairs using index cards. Companies such as Pro Lingua Associates and others publish books for teachers detailing many specific language-learning activities using index cards.

ESL instruction relative to how much teachers should talk and giving positive endings to classes

ESL teachers must be careful not to be the ones talking most of the time in class. The teacher never should be speaking in class more than the students (combined) speak, except with groups at the very lowest levels of English language development. Even ESL students with higher English proficiency levels are not speaking their native languages, so it is not natural or comfortable for them to speak English. They are likely to get insufficient practice if the teacher is speaking more of the time. ESL educators find it helpful to end each class on a positive note by giving students a sense of accomplishment through positive reinforcement and encouragement. They also find it helps to end ESL classes with a joke, funny story, or game, so students take away a pleasant experience and look forward to the next class, rather than leaving feeling discouraged at not achieving perfect English overnight and how much they still have to learn, which can cause aversion to future classes and undermine their motivation.

Monitoring individual ESL students' learning progress and problems

One strategy that teachers of ESL students can use to obtain mutually beneficial feedback is regularly assigning all students to write the teacher a letter stating what they have learned, what they still need and/or want to learn, and what is confusing to them. Teachers benefit from the specific information about each student's progress and needs and by receiving feedback from each student's individual perspective. Teachers also can identify patterns in a class when multiple students give similar feedback about certain aspects of what they are and are not learning. Furthermore, teachers can use this knowledge to improve their instruction on a continual basis. The ESL students always benefit from receiving personal responses from their teacher. The students also benefit from the more individualized instruction the teacher can give them based on their feedback. The teacher can use this information to capitalize on individual students' strengths and focus more intensive instruction on areas in which they have deficits or confusion.

Incomplete stories, Bingo games, and scrambled word games

Some teachers read obscure fairy tales or other stories to their ESL students, omitting the ending. The students then must supply an ending, which they determine by asking questions probing for more information. One variation involves restricting questions to those with "yes/no" answers. This method enhances students' listening comprehension, spoken English, question construction, sense of plot structure, learning engagement, imagination, and fun. Many teachers also use Bingo to give English-language reinforcement and practice. With beginning ESLs, some teachers limit Bingo letters to vowels, giving students practice in recognizing/differentiating English vowel sounds and also the numbers used, while they have fun. Another technique involves writing a fairly long (9-10 letters) scrambled word on the board and having students, as a class or in small groups, see how many 1-letter, 2-letter, 3-letter, etc. words they can make from its letters. This method also challenges each student to unscramble the original word. This game can last from 5-45 minutes and helps build vocabulary.

Expanding ESL students' vocabulary, syntactic, and grammatical learning when presenting words

Experienced teachers recommend that whenever the teacher presents a word to ESL students, s/he should expand on it. For example, when presenting nouns, the teacher can include their plural forms, and mass nouns related to count nouns, e.g. letter, letters, mail. When presenting verbs, the teacher can include which prepositions it can take, e.g. to talk to, about, with, over, around, etc., and explain (or ask non-beginner students to explain) how each preposition affects the word's meaning. Another technique involves using graphic visual reminders. For example, a common error among ESL students is failing to add the final "s" to third-person singular present-tense verbs and/or to plural nouns. The teacher can keep on hand a large letter "S" of cardboard, plastic, or other durable material, and hold it up (silently) whenever a student omits an "s" while speaking. A variation involves having students pass the "S" to other students making this error. Using the visual modality reinforces and supplements auditory instruction in speaking English.

Significance of the teacher's movements in ESL instruction

ESL teachers should realize that not only their words, but also their movements transmit considerable meaning. Researchers have found that in a presentation, only 10% of its impact comes from words, 30% comes from the presenter's voice, and 60% comes from movement. The definition of movement includes the teacher's appearance, facial expressions, posture, gestures, and other body language. Because verbal and analytical activities are performed in the brain's left hemisphere, many instructional activities focus on operations using the left hemisphere. However, educators advise including activities that also use the right hemisphere, e.g. music, art, creative work, visualization, imagination, dance, and other spatial and kinetic functions. Using multiple modalities strengthens learning, exercises both sides of the brain, and provides balance, variety, and enjoyment. It also affords ESL students access to learning in English via avenues other than already knowing English. Students not only love singing, it also reinforces English sounds and intonational patterns. Teachers also can make partial/unfinished/ambiguous drawings, which students must complete and then write about them.

Games that combines use of spoken English, listening comprehension, and drawing

Some ESL teachers have devised games to give students practice in speaking and listening in English, combined with drawing. For example, two students sit back to back so they cannot see one another or the materials they hold. One student is given a picture containing abstract figures; the other is given blank paper and pencil. The student holding the picture must describe in English the sizes, locations, and shapes of the abstract forms; the other student must try to draw what the first student describes. By taking turns, each student gets practice using spoken English to describe specific properties, and practice understanding English speech, interpreting it, and following directions. Adding the element of drawing engages the brain's right hemisphere, balancing the left hemisphere's verbal and analytical functions, and reinforcing verbal learning and giving students another modality through which they can apprehend English as a new language.

Questionnaire instruments

Scholars including those studying area linguistics, sociology, cultural anthropology, and history have long used questionnaires to collect oral history from informants. This method is invaluable for gathering information from illiterate informants. It is equally useful with literate informants for eliciting a wealth of detailed personal history. The conversational format stimulates more recollections, disclosures and expressions. These questionnaires, available from local public libraries and universities, have the same effect of stimulating conversation and discussion with ESL students. For example, they include items such as describing one's childhood home, including layout, rooms, and sleeping arrangements; how and/or which members of the family shopped, cooked, served, ate, cleaned up after meals; how they did laundry; what jobs family members had; memories of childhood experiences, e.g. times they had the most fun, the worst trouble they got into; family pets, etc. Speaking an unfamiliar, non-native language is easier for ESL students when the subject matter is familiar and personal to them. Discovering similarities and differences with other students' backgrounds also stimulates interest and discussion.

Using a content-based ESL curriculum in school

ESL students typically are significantly behind mainstream students in the background knowledge they need to access regular academic instruction in English. However, educators and researchers find that teaching content areas such as social studies, math, and the sciences at the normal grade level helps ESL students to catch up on this background knowledge, making learning easier when they join mainstream classes. Research shows ESL students appreciate the challenges of content-based curriculum and its higher standards, and they feel more prepared for mainstream classes by their enhanced understanding. As a result, content-based ESL curricula (CBEC) motivate students. CBEC use authentic content subject textbooks rather than artificial and/or simplistic ESL-only texts, making learning more contextual and meaningful. Learning English in the process of, and as a means for, learning science/other academic subjects makes English learning more purposeful, which reciprocally can speed up English acquisition. CBEC also address a crucial need: namely, ESL student's lack of technical vocabulary in academic subjects. Learning and using technical vocabulary in context makes the knowledge more lasting.

Normal stages of native/first-language literacy development

Typically, when parents read aloud to children, babies aged 6-12 months pay attention to pictures in books and touch or pat them with their hands. They recognize familiar objects in pictures and prefer pictures of faces to pictures of objects. They vocalize and attempt to turn pages with parental assistance. From 12-18 months, they can turn pages themselves, hold and carry books, and ask parents to read to them. They can turn a book the right way to view it. They learn that words have meanings. They will point to pictured objects in books and verbally name them. Children's expressive vocabulary begins emerging at this age; they usually utter their first words from 10-14 months old. By 18 months, children typically can utter 20-100 words and begin to scribble on paper. They try to imitate parents by "reading" aloud; they can recite familiar passages, and fill in words parents omit. Their attention spans are inconsistent at this age. They understand the concept that printed language is a symbol.

By the time children are 2 years old, their expressive vocabularies have reached about 300 words. They develop early abilities to express narratives: "Heaps," i.e. groups of simple statements and unrelated ideas emerge, as do sequences, i.e. narratives including a central character, setting, or topic. When parents read aloud to them, 2-3-year-olds show emergent comprehension of the concept of plot. They learn to turn paper pages in regular books. They look for their favorite pictures in books and can connect the text to the pictures. They will practice "reading" to themselves. They can recite phrases they remember from books read aloud to them, and some may even recite whole stories. If the parent reading aloud says a wrong word, they will object. Some children will correct the error with the right word. Other children may not remember the correct word, but they still might notice an incorrect word and point it out to parents.

By 3 years old, children typically have developed spoken vocabularies of 900 words. They begin to tell simple narratives. Their scribbling starts to resemble letters, and some children can write series of letters. By age 4, they place more importance on the plots of stories their parents read to them. They can turn paper book pages one at a time. They still enjoy hearing repeated readings of familiar books, and they also become able to attend to longer books read aloud. They can follow or track the text now, and they begin to recognize specific letters. They can recount stories familiar to them. At this age they also begin to "write" their own names. Another new development in literacy for children aged 3-4 years is the ability to rhyme words spontaneously. Significant also is the emergence of print awareness in children between 3 and 4 years of age.

Between the ages of 3 and 4 years, in addition to the growth of vocabulary, simple narrative ability, and early writing, children also develop print awareness. They become interested in the printed words and numbers on signs and labels. They may identify some books by their covers and be able to name their titles. They look not only at the pictures, but also the text in books, and they now grasp the front-to-back and left-to-right orientations of reading books printed in English. They may identify some letters and numbers at this age. Some children in this stage of literacy development understand the concept that people can use writing as a means of communicating. Some highly literate parents who have always read to their children have observed that when they read to their young children, who are usually quite advanced in their intelligence and language development, the children will even start reading words back to them at these ages.

By the age of 4 years, most children have speaking vocabularies of about 1500 words. By the age of 5, most children have developed expressive vocabularies of 2500 words. In spoken narratives, they develop "unfocused chains," i.e. stories that connect events through causal or logical relationships but have no main character or topic. Children at 4-5 years expand on the skills they developed at ages 3-4 years. Their print awareness progresses in recognizing letters, telling them apart, and writing/copying them. They typically learn to write their own names. Some begin rudimentary keyboard typing. They will make stories or notes on paper combining letters, drawings, and scribbling. They now can recognize rhymes when they hear them. Phonologically, they can separate and count the syllables within words. Some children aged 4-5 years will try to spell words that they hear and speak, though it is also normal for this ability to emerge later, at up to 7 years of age.

Children begin reading independently around the age of 5 years, and they master this skill around the age of 7 years. They also develop the motivation to read independently during this period. They begin to identify with characters in the books that they read. They develop personal reading preferences for particular literary genres. Having attained phonological and print awareness earlier, they now can apply these skills to understanding the alphabetic principle. For example, they can change letters in words that they hear or read to form different words, e.g. "cat-hat-bat-mat-sat-fat." Whereas they previously had recognized words as visual wholes or gestalts, now they can associate the initial and final letters in words with their corresponding speech sounds to "read" them. They begin to learn the conventions of writing and spelling. By the time a typical child is around 5 years of age, s/he will have developed an expressive vocabulary of about 2500 words.

Children aged 9 years and older normally already will have mastered the ability to read autonomously and will begin to read progressively more difficult material, including more advanced vocabulary, longer books, more complex plots, more extensive casts of characters, additional literary genres, longer compound and complex sentences, and higher-level and more abstract concepts. Children at this stage begin to understand what qualities make them unique individuals. As they approach their teen years, they become occupied with asserting their independence. This quest for independence is reflected in their choices of reading matter and fueled by the ideas they are inspired to form through reading and writing. They further develop their critical thinking skills. This development, together with the need to become independent, enables young people to question authority rather than blindly accepting or slavishly following its dictates. As Piaget showed, children become capable of abstract thought and can understand concepts such as justice, liberty, patriotism, and ethical principles. They are also better able to understand others' perspectives on higher levels, thereby enabling altruistic/prosocial behaviors.

Hallmarks of literacy development observed

Children's ability to rhyme words independently first emerges around the ages of 3-4 years. They develop the ability to identify rhymes when they hear them soon thereafter, at around 4-5 years old. Between the ages of 5 and 7 years, they can generate their own rhymes, and also become able to categorize rhymes and make judgments about them. Whereas younger children, aged 4-5 years, can expressively deliver "unfocused chain" narratives, which follow a logical or cause-and-effect sequence but have no main character or topic, children aged 5-7 years develop "focused chain" narratives. These are stories they tell that include both a logical sequence of events and also a primary character. At this stage, children's focused chain narratives take on the structure of serial "adventures." Phonologically, children aged 5-7 develop the abilities to combine or blend phonemes (speech sounds); to count the phonemes in words; to identify the initial, middle, and final phonemes in words; and to delete and substitute phonemes. They also begin using phonetic spelling.

Approved Educator Standards of English Language Arts and Reading

For teaching certification in grades 4-8 English Language Arts and Reading, Standard I: Oral Language requires beginning teachers to know and understand the importance and developmental processes of spoken language and to give students varied opportunities for developing listening and speaking skills. Standard II: Foundations of Reading requires teachers to comprehend the bases of early literacy development and reading. Standard III: Word Analysis Skills and Reading Fluency requires teachers to understand the significance of such student word analysis skills as decoding, blending, sight word vocabulary, structural analysis, and reading fluency and to offer students plenty of opportunities to improve and practice these skills. Standard IV: Reading Comprehension states that beginning Language Arts and Reading teachers of grades 4-8 in Texas must realize how and why it is important for students to understand what they read. Teachers also must know the individual parts of reading comprehension and teach their students strategies to improve their reading comprehension.

To obtain teacher certification in Language Arts and Reading for grades 4-8 in Texas, Standard V: Written Language dictates that beginning teachers must understand writing as a developmental process. Therefore, this standard also states that teachers must give their students instruction that assists them in developing competencies for communicating in writing. The Texas State Board of Educator Certification (SBEC)'s Standard VI: Study and Inquiry Skills addresses the significance of students' developing skills for questioning, examining, investigating, and researching academic and real-life topics and skills for effective studying of school subjects; thus, teachers must realize the significance of these skills and foster students' development and application of these skills as learning tools. Standard VII: Viewing and Representing requires teachers to know how to analyze, interpret, evaluate, and produce visual messages and images using different media and give students opportunities to develop these skills. Standard VIII: Assessment of Developing Literacy requires teachers to understand basic assessment principles and to apply varied ways of assessing literacy in planning and delivering instruction.

Texas SBEC for teachers of Language Arts and Reading to students in grades 8-12

In the Texas State Board of Educator Certification (SBEC)'s Approved Educator Standards for grades 8-12 Language Arts and Reading, Standard I requires beginning teachers to be able to design and deliver instruction that reflects knowledge of the Texas Essential Knowledge and Skills (TEKS); is right for each student; integrates all parts—listening, speaking, reading, writing, and viewing/representing—of the English language arts; and is founded upon a continuous assessment process. Standard II requires teachers of language arts to understand the processes involved in reading and to teach their students how to apply these processes. Standard III requires teachers additionally to understand the skills needed and strategies to use in reading different kinds of non-literary text materials and to teach students how to apply these skills and strategies to improve lifetime learning. Standard IV requires teachers to understand a broad range of literary genres and a large body of literary works, to give students opportunities to see literature as a resource for exploration and interpretation of human experience, and to read a variety of literature types.

Standard V of Texas' SBEC teacher certification standards in English Language Arts and Reading for grades 8-12 requires that teachers realize writing as process an ongoing, developmental, integrative, and recursive process. In addition, teachers must offer students opportunities to develop writing competency. Standard VI requires middle and high school Language Arts and Reading teachers to understand ways of producing effective writing for diverse audiences and to offer students ways to develop and practice their writing skills in varied contexts and formats. Standard VII stipulates that middle and high school Language Arts and Reading teachers understand the history and structure of the English language and offer students ways of acquiring associated knowledge and skills within contexts meaningful to them. Standard VIII requires that Language Arts and Reading teachers of grades 8-12 understand oral communication and furnish students with chances to develop listening and speaking skills. Standard IX says these teachers must be able to analyze, interpret, and create visual messages and images in diverse media and afford students ways to develop these skills.

TEKS for Spanish Language Arts and Reading in elementary and secondary schools

The Spanish Language Arts TEKS reflect standards authentic to Spanish literacy and language rather than simply being translations from English. The Spanish TEKS cite consistent research findings that learning in English as an L2 (second language) is improved by literacy development in the L1 (first/native language). Cognitive development, learning, and achievement progress best when students understand the language of instruction. Moreover, when students develop strong literacy skills in L1, they transfer them to English as they learn it, affecting faster progress with learning in the English language. Despite the surface appearance of many similarities between Spanish and English in alphabets, spelling, and vocabulary cognates, each language still has different conventions for which the reading process in that language is a prerequisite. This makes it crucial to give systematic instruction in the needed skills, following the correct order for skills acquisition. Recent research shows that students use their L1 literacy knowledge in learning L2 literacy. How well students learn via formal Spanish instruction predicts how much they will transfer to English.

TEKS standards for Spanish Language Arts and Reading for all grade levels

The Texas Essential Skills and Knowledge (TEKS) for Spanish Language Arts and Reading include these strands: Reading–students read and understand a broad range of informational and literary texts. This strand is organized to reflect pertinent current research results on Spanish literacy development, including the chief subject areas of the National Reading Panel Report. Writing–students write varied texts, each having a clear main idea, appropriate organization, and sufficient detail. Research–students know how to find various pertinent sources, can evaluate information and ideas, synthesize them, and present them to others. Listening and Speaking–students in groups and conversations listen to others' ideas, respond to them, and share their own thoughts. Oral and Written Conventions–students learn how to use the practices of Spanish language in their speech and writing. Kindergarteners should be read to daily; elementary and middle school grades should be read to and read and write daily. High school, in addition to Spanish, has TEKS standards for English I and II for Speakers of Other Languages (ESOL).

TEKS regarding the English-language proficiency levels of ESOL students in high school

Not only do individual ESOL students vary in their English-language proficiency levels, but within the individual student levels of proficiency in different English-language components vary. For example, one student might exhibit an advanced level of oral English expression, an intermediate level of English reading, and a beginning level of English writing. For students to access the curriculum, teachers must know these individual student proficiency levels. These levels dictate linguistic instructional accommodations that will enable students to learn academic content such as translations and texts adapted to proficiency level, and scaffolding (support) needed such as bilingual dictionary, thesaurus, glossaries, pictures, real objects, etc. The opportunities each student has for linguistic interactions inside and outside school will influence his/her proficiency levels in each component area and overall. The TEKS identify ESOL high school students' English-language proficiency levels as Beginning, Intermediate, Advanced, and High Advanced.

Fundamental ways the Spanish language differs from English with respect to spelling, pronunciation, and reading

In Spanish, words are spelled the way they are pronounced and vice versa much more consistently than in English. (Consider that in English rough, though, through and bough, the letter combination -ough is pronounced four different ways with the same spelling, and none of these pronunciations matches that spelling.) Because the look and sound of Spanish words correspond more, the syllable is a more important phonological awareness unit and predicts successful Spanish reading. English learning employs sight word recognition because many English words cannot be decoded for sound based on their irregular spellings (e.g. are, one or the –ough words above); Spanish does not use sight words because decoding is straightforward due to its more transparent spelling. Thus, Spanish students learn to decode faster and soon move on to comprehension and fluency. Spanish instruction employs most frequently used words rather than sight words. Comprehension is a more significant issue in Spanish than decoding. Such linguistic features inform the methods and development of reading instruction.

Skills identified by the TEKS for high school ELL students at the Beginning and Intermediate levels of English-language proficiency

Beginning ELL students can find meaning associated with spoken English through making inferences about text, visuals, actions, vocal tones, and intonational patterns. They attain some receptive English comprehension first. Then they produce oral English to express meaning and develop increasing fluency and accuracy. They use their previous knowledge of language, text structure, text context, written phonic cues, other visual information, and syntax to read English. ELL students at the Intermediate level enhance their English comprehension and speaking skills through the listening process. By communicating in meaningful interactions, they differentiate, clarify, and evaluate ideas in diverse circumstances and contexts. They succeed at participating in social, academic, and work settings by speaking English to generate concepts and to clarify, evaluate, and critique them. They use their English vocabulary development to improve their listening and reading comprehension, and they can write English text to address various purposes and audiences.

Skills that are identified for ELL high school students at the Advanced and High Advanced English-language proficiency levels by the TEKS

According to the TEKS, students at the Advanced proficiency level actively extend their English vocabulary by using their more developed listening skills. They use this vocabulary expansion to analyze and evaluate oral English applying to varied purposes and situations. They use spoken English to interact in diverse situations, producing, clarifying, evaluating, and critiquing ideas. Advanced ELL students constantly develop their reading skills further in order to increase proficiency in reading text specific to academic content-area subjects for various purposes. They produce written text in various modalities and addressing varied audiences. They communicate meanings commensurate with their respective proficiency levels. The TEKS say students at the High Advanced proficiency level read, write, listen, and speak comparably to native English-speaking students. They comprehend grade-level English used in academic and social contexts. They possess and apply grade-level English-language skills in academic subjects and effectively use content-based and abstract vocabulary. They continually build skills for fluency, prosody, and higher-order comprehension as reading foundations. They write at grade level and use strong mastery of English linguistic structures.

Reading knowledge and skills identified by the TEKS for ESOL II students in high school in the areas of Comprehension of Literary Text for Theme and Genre, Poetry, and Drama

For comprehending themes and genres in literary texts, the TEKS expect high school ESOL II students to compare and contrast related themes set in different historical periods; to analyze archetypes such as a tragic flaw or a hero's journey in mythological, classical, and traditional literature; and to correlate a literary work's cultural and historical context with its associated figurative language. The TEKS expect high school ESL students to understand the structure and elements of poetry and drama, to make inferences and draw conclusions about these, and to support this understanding by supplying evidence from the text. Students also are expected to analyze prosody (rhyme scheme, meter) in poetry, other structure, and its graphic elements (word positioning, punctuation, line length). In reading drama, TEKS expect students to analyze the ways in which the motifs and archetypes used influence a play's plot.

What the TEKS expect ESOL II students in high school to do to demonstrate reading comprehension of Expository, Persuasive, and Procedural forms of informational text

In reading informational text, the TEKS expect high school ELL students to summarize expository text, differentiate summaries from critiques, and identify non-essential information in summaries and unsupported opinions in critiques; differentiate empirical, logical, anecdotal and other types of evidence supporting arguments and conclusions in text; draw complex conclusions and subtle inferences

- 85 -

about ideas and their structural patterns in text and defend these conclusions and inferences; and synthesize and logically relate ideas and details from multiple texts reflecting various perspectives on one topic, including textual support. With persuasive text, students are expected to evaluate evidence supporting arguments for accuracy and explain perspective shifts within arguments on the same topic and to analyze current political debates for false dilemmas, personal attacks, appeals to pity, appeals to common opinions, and other logical and rhetorical fallacies. With procedural text, students are expected to evaluate the visual appeal and clarity of graphics in text and to synthesize information from maps, charts, schematics and other graphic sources in order to draw conclusions about the ideas these convey.

Knowledge and skills required by the TEKS for high school ESOL II students for Reading in the area of Vocabulary Development

The TEKS require ESOL II students in high school to comprehend and apply new English vocabulary that they learn in reading and writing, including: (1) ascertaining the meaning of grade-level academic technical terms in English for subjects such as social studies, mathematics, the sciences, and the arts using roots, prefixes, and suffixes from Greek, Latin, and other languages; (2) analyzing the context of sentences and passages of text to differentiate between the denotations and connotations of word meanings; (3) identifying and analyzing word relationships such as analogies to infer word meanings; (4) demonstrating the relationships between the foreign origins of words/phrases commonly used in English and the associated historical events (e.g. coup d'état, avant-garde, perestroika, glasnost); (5) ascertaining or verifying the definitions, denotations, connotations, and etymology of English words or phrases by using a printed or electronic glossary, dictionary, or thesaurus.

TEKS expectations of ESOL II students

Reading areas of Comprehension of Literary Text

Students must demonstrate understanding, inferences, conclusions, and supporting textual evidence regarding fiction's structure and elements; literary nonfiction's various structural features and patterns; sensory language's creation of imagery; and the author's purpose in cultural, historical, and contemporary contexts. In literary fiction, the TEKS expect students to analyze scenes and the scene's respective impact on plot success in various works; analyze variations in fictional characters' moral dilemmas across cultures or nations; evaluate relationships between narrative forms and tones; and show familiarity with works and authors from non-English-speaking literary traditions, especially 20th-century world literature. In literary nonfiction, the TEKS expect students to judge the roles of voice, tone, imagery, diction, and syntax in essays, speeches, etc. Regarding sensory language, the TEKS expect students to articulate the functions of allusions, symbolism, and allegories and how an author's use of sensory description creates imagery. Regarding culture and history, the TEKS expect students to analyze the particular purpose of a text passage, its controlling idea, and its supportive and elaborative elements, including most important and less important details.

Writing for Oral and Written Conventions
The TEKS expect ESOL II students to understand and apply academic conventions in their writing and speech and develop more complexity in applying previously learned standards. In addition, they are expected to understand and use: more complex active and passive verb tenses and verbals such as infinitives, participles, and gerunds; reciprocal pronouns (one another, each other); restrictive and nonrestrictive relative clauses and the difference between them; the subjunctive mood for expressing possibilities, wishes, and doubts; and compound, complex, and compound-complex sentences with correct structure. The TEKS also expect ESOL II students to write legibly and correctly apply the conventions of capitalization and punctuation in their written compositions. They are expected to understand and correctly place commas in nonrestrictive clauses, phrases, and expressions of contrast; to show irony or sarcasm by correctly placing quotation marks; and to emphasize parenthetical information with the correct placement of dashes. Students are also expected to spell English words correctly and use various resources to determine or verify correct spelling.

Second Language Acquisition regarding reading
The expectations of the TEKS for ESOL II students in Second Language Acquisition/Reading include: Learning English sound-letter relationships, identifying roots, base words, affixes, and cognates and sounding out/decoding words; recognizing top-bottom and left-right English reading directionality; developing basic sight vocabulary including English structures commonly used in both classroom materials and environmental print; using graphic organizers, illustrations, pre-learned topic-related vocabulary, and other pre-reading supports to aid comprehension; reading materials with progressively fewer linguistic accommodations as they learn English; comprehending progressively more difficult English through developing background knowledge and vocabulary, understanding English structures, and reading grade-level content-area text with teacher, peer, contextual, and visual support. Students are expected to read silently for longer durations with progressing ease. The TEKS also expect them to show comprehension of progressively more complex English through shared reading participation, summarizing/retelling material, answering questions, and taking notes appropriately according to the demands of content area subjects and grade levels.

The TEKS expect ESOL II students to demonstrate proficiency of second-language acquisition in reading by expanding their English reading skills and comprehension. Students show they understand supporting ideas and details in textual and graphic materials, summarize text they read, and differentiate main concepts from details according to the demands of academic content areas. Students must use inferential skills including making predictions, relating ideas, making conclusions and inferences based on textual and graphic sources, and locating evidence in text accordingly with the demands of content area subjects. They must be able to make critical analyses and evaluate written information according to grade-level and content-area needs by using analytical skills. To understand progressively harder English, they must develop background knowledge, vocabulary, and linguistic structures through reading authentic literature and using kinesthetic visual supports. Students must use verbal (intonations, pauses) and nonverbal (facial expressions, gestures) cues to enhance reading. They can retell, act out, and/or visually illustrate event sequences from text they read. ELLs fulfill these expectations at their own English proficiency levels.

Second Language Acquisition in the area of Writing
At their own individual English proficiency levels, TEKS expect ESOL II students to write in various forms with progressing accuracy in language arts and content-area subjects for various audiences and purposes. This expectation includes writing that incorporates newly learned basic and content-area vocabulary at the students' respective grade levels. Such ability also demonstrates an increase in students' spelling accuracy through knowing and using English spelling rules and patterns and editing their writing for grade-level, standard usage, and grammar, including using correct verb tenses, subject-verb agreement, and pronoun agreement. In addition, students use progressively greater complexity of grammar structures in grade-level content-area writing including the correct use of the nominative, objective, and possessive cases, negatives, contractions, parts of speech, auxiliary verbs, etc. TEKS also expect students to write varied sentence lengths and patterns and combine phrases and clauses with connecting words appropriate to their grade levels and with progressing accuracy as they acquire more English language knowledge.

Included in the TEKS ESOL II student expectations in second-language acquisition regarding writing is the students' ability to describe, narrate, and explain in their writing with greater detail and precision in order to meet the demands of writing in the academic content area subjects. Students are expected to capitalize and punctuate correctly, including capitalizing initial letters of first names and first words in sentences and correctly using periods, exclamation points, and question marks. The TEKS expect ESOL II students to use graphic organizers as pre-writing activities to define their previous knowledge, incorporate newly added information, and prepare for writing. ESOL II students are expected to demonstrate greater proficiency in using patterns of orthography such as s- consonant blends (str-, spl-, etc.), digraphs, and rules including u following q; doubling consonants and y-to-i conversion for past tenses (-ed); and dropping final e's with -ing suffixes. Students also are expected to classify ideas and organize them into sentences and paragraphs in developing drafts for written work..

Practice Test

Practice Questions

1. Second language instruction research indicates that second language learners typically absorb _____ and then use them in understanding _____.
    a. rules of the language; idiomatic expressions
    b. formulaic expressions; rules of the language
    c. idiomatic expressions; rules of the language
    d. rules of grammar; figurative language

2. In 1963, the first two-way immersion (TWI) program in the United States was established. Between then and the early 90s, the growth of TWI programs throughout the country was
    a. exponential, nearly doubling every two to three years
    b. static, with fewer than a dozen documented programs
    c. steady, gaining an average of 10 new programs per year
    d. uneven; twenty programs were established in the first decade, 37 in the next five years and 120 in the final five years

3. Dr. Wu has paired his ELLs with native English-speaking partners after they have read a chapter from a text. He has given each pair a specific task related to the text, and each member of each pair has received additional information that is unique, or that differs somewhat from information the partner has received. The students are asked to examine, discuss, and complete the task together. This approach is an example of
    a. shared-information tasks
    b. two-heads-are-better-than-one tasks
    c. multiple-approaches tasks
    d. information-gap tasks

4. This Federal Act of 1964, also known as Title VI, set the stage for equal opportunity in education by giving all students the right to meaningful, effective instruction.
    a. Bilingual Education Act
    b. Brown v. Board of Education
    c. Civil Rights Act
    d. Equal Opportunities Act

5. A second grader was in the United States for part of her kindergarten school year. Her family returned to Mexico partway through the year. She attended first grade in Mexico. Now, her family has returned to Texas. Does she meet TAKS immigrant status requirements?

    a. Yes, as long as she's attended school outside the U.S. for at least one year.

    b. No, because she gave up that status when her family returned to Mexico.

    c. Yes, as long as she's lived outside the U.S. for at least two full years. She lived in Mexico for the first four years of her life, so she meets the requirements.

    d. No, because she has not lived outside the United States for two consecutive years.

6. Syntax, vocabulary and concepts that have been well-integrated and are employed consistently in informal communication, and that develop in ELLs within the first 2–3 years of exposure to the new language are

    a. CALPS

    b. BICS

    c. ICLS

    d. ISC

7. A parent has approached her son's second-grade teacher with the concern that, since the classroom is bilingual and instruction is given in both English and Spanish, the students will experience a delay in learning English. What does the teacher explain to the parent?

    a. Her fears are somewhat justified. In fact, students in bilingual classrooms do not initially develop an enriched facility with English at the same rate as do monolingual learners; however, over time, they surpass these learners.

    b. Her fears are somewhat justified. In fact, students in bilingual classrooms initially develop linguistic facility in English at a somewhat advanced rate. But unless English is spoken outside of school such advantages may be lost. Therefore, it is important for the parent to work with the teacher in advancing her son's language skills.

    c. Her fears, while understandable, are not supported by research. In fact, students in bilingual classrooms achieve linguistic facility at about the same rate, and have advantages in terms of more specialized knowledge in some areas.

    d. Her fears, while understandable, are not supported by research. In fact, students in bilingual classrooms achieve linguistic facility faster than students in monolingual classrooms.

8. What assessment tool, designed with consideration of TELPAS, is used exclusively to evaluate ELLs' reading improvement?

    a. ELLR

    b. RPTE

    c. R2D2

    d. TRIA

9. Is it more important for second-language instruction to focus on the intended meaning of a message or the grammatical form that message takes?
    a. grammatical form, because until a speaker understands the rules of a language, he will not be able to communicate effectively
    b. grammatical form, because it is easy to memorize a few forms then plug in vocabulary as appropriate to express a wide variety of meanings
    c. meaning, because ELLs are better able to decode messages and they encode their own ideas best when they are motivated by the desire and actively attempting to communicate something meaningful
    d. meaning, because when actively communicating to another, the ELL can indicate environmental context by pointing, miming or demonstrating

10. An ELL student goes to a school with a large population of students who are L2 learners. Many are Spanish speakers, and there is also a significant Korean population as well as a number of students from Vietnam. The ELL spends between two and three hours a day in a class where content area instruction is offered in English, and the remainder of the time in a resource center with other L2 learners for English Language instruction. What type of program is he participating in?
    a. two-way immersion
    b. sheltered English
    c. English as a Second Language
    d. early exit bilingual program

11. What is the NCELA and what are its stated purposes?
    a. Natural Concepts in English Language Assessments; "We strive to provide an assessment series for bilingual teachers that combines the best of current research with tried and true methods for a naturalized system that is both easy to use and easy to interpret."
    b. National Clearinghouse for English Language Acquisition; "To collect, coordinate and convey a broad range of research and resources in support of an inclusive approach to high quality education for ELLs."
    c. Necessary Concepts in the Education of Linguistic Altruism; "To research, disseminate and advise world communities about the importance of preserving and respecting all languages in order to foster world peace and academic excellence from which all can equally benefit."
    d. No Child's Education in English is Academic; "Children learn by direct experience. We must teach ELLs, as well as children whose primary language is English but who lack sufficient language skills, in intuitive ways that will stimulate the imagination."

12. A K–4th minority-language dominant TWI program is
    a. one in which the minority language is employed instructionally at least 80% of the time
    b. one in which the minority language is employed instructionally at least 40% of the time
    c. one in which the majority language is employed approximately 48% of the time
    d. one in which the majority language is employed at least 80% of the time

13. What principles are essential for the successful integration of content and language instruction?
    a. Students should be grouped heterogeneously; instruction should be given in both first and second languages; lessons are divided into a language component and a content component; error should be corrected on the spot.
    b. Lessons are divided into a language component and content component; there is daily review of the previous lesson; lessons build upon one another; outcomes are continuously observed and assessed.
    c. Students should be grouped homogeneously; instruction should be given in both first and second languages; lessons are divided into a language component and a content component; error should be corrected on the spot.
    d. There are planned outcomes for both content and language learning; goal-oriented interaction takes place; tasks that advance listening, speaking, reading and writing are integrated; outcomes are continuously observed and assessed.

14. Code-switching is
    a. switching the order of words in a second language according to the syntax of a first language
    b. slipping back and forth between two languages
    c. switching around letters or syllables to result in gibberish; for example, 'ageslange' instead of 'languages'
    d. switching both syllables and stress to result in another word; for example, 'parade' instead of 'rapid'

15. In Spanish, alphabetic letters represent a single phonemic sound; therefore, anyone who knows the sounds associated with the letters can determine pronunciation based upon the letters. Is it logical to assume that an orally produced word will have a single, predictable spelling?
    a. Yes; thus if pronunciation is regular, then spelling must be regular, as well.
    b. No, spelling and pronunciation are not perfectly aligned.
    c. It cannot be determined by the information provided.
    d. Yes, both spelling and pronunciation in Spanish are intimately and perfectly matched.

16. What are the four principles of classroom instructional practice required for the convergence of content areas and instruction in English?

    a. Instructional practices must be vertical, depending upon previous instruction and prior knowledge. Each lesson gives equal importance to content learning and language learning through drills, graphic organizers and manipulatives. Lessons are repetitive but not redundant. Students are encouraged to ask questions, and to answer one another's questions while the teacher listens and assesses.

    b. Each lesson is designed to result in specific content and language learning goals. Lessons encourage students to communicate with other members of the classroom and the teacher in order to achieve specific skills and understanding related to the content. The teacher offers tasks that encourage all language skills—listening, speaking, writing and reading within content areas. Ongoing results within the learning process are noted and assessed as part of the lesson.

    c. Lessons within one content area are designed to converge with all other lessons to be taught on the same day through repetitive themes. Lessons encourage students to communicate with other members of the classroom and the teacher in order to achieve specific skills and understanding related to the content. Lessons are repetitive but not redundant. Students are encouraged to ask questions, and to answer one another's questions while the teacher listens and assesses.

    d. Each lesson is designed to result in specific content and language learning goals, which are set by the students themselves. Lessons encourage students to work independently and individually until the end of the lesson time. At that point, students come together to communicate with other members of the classroom and the teacher orally, with graphic organizers or by reading pieces of their own writing aloud. Ongoing results within the learning process are noted and assessed as part of the lesson.

17. Cultural Orientation refers to

    a. exposure to the high arts from a variety of countries

    b. educating American-born students about the cultures of their non-native classmates

    c. educating immigrants in terms of cultural mores, necessary skills and knowledge

    d. educating non-native students about the culture of their American-born classmates

18. The five sections of the Language Assessment Scales (LAS) are sound/phrase recognition, sound/phrase reproduction, vocabulary, comprehension and

    a. syntactical awareness

    b. semantic use

    c. syntactical complexity

    d. story retelling

19. Two-way immersion and English as a second language programs share a number of things in common. What is one difference?

    a. ESL programs are held in self-contained classrooms; TWI programs are pull-outs.

    b. ESL students lose facility with their original language, while those in TWI programs don't lose facility while learning English.

    c. ESL students remain in class with native English speakers for the entire day, and are instructed exclusively in English.

    d. TWI students lose facility with their original language, while those in ESL programs don't lose facility while learning English.

20. As mandated by Title III of the No Child Left Behind Act, states must determine Annual Measurable Achievement Objectives that suggest the level of English proficiency Title III-funded students should gain each year. What three areas of reporting are specifically required?

    a. For each year, each state is required to report: increases in the percentage of students making progress in learning English; increases in percentage of students achieving English proficiency; ELL students making Adequate Yearly Progress.

    b. The state must report overall increases or decreases in numbers of: LEP students both from the previous year and since 1995; students who have graduated out of the program because they have achieved fluency; students who have left the program because they quit school or the family has moved.

    c. There is no such requirement.

    d. States are requested but not required to report increases in the percentage of students making progress in learning English; increases in percentage of students achieving English proficiency; ELL students making Adequate Yearly Progress.

21. Formative assessments are used to

    a. record instruction

    b. improve teaching methods

    c. design and implement instruction

    d. review instruction

22. The four language modalities are

    a. Spanish, English, French, Chinese

    b. listening, speaking, reading, writing

    c. semantics, syntax, vocabulary, context

    d. reading, writing, math, science

23. Ms. Hernandez is planning a reading lesson for her first graders. She is using an integrated content and language approach. She knows she must design the lesson around specific desired outcomes in the areas of both language and content, but is struggling with how to do so. Which of the following approaches will serve her best?

    a. Clarify her goals by writing them down, using descriptive verbs such as 'discuss, listen, ask, point out' and 'demonstrate.'

    b. Clarify her goals by considering the desired outcomes.

    c. Clarify her desired outcomes by fine-tuning the results.

    d. Clarify her goals by discussing them with the students.

24. What is the difference between implicit and explicit knowledge?

    a. Implicit knowledge is all knowledge that each communicator subconsciously believes is shared knowledge between all speakers in a communication event. Explicit knowledge is all knowledge that is conscientiously communicated to assure all parties that they are communicating about the same thing.

    b. Implicit knowledge involves an unspoken agreement between speakers, who are complicit with one another; implicit knowledge is privately held between one and a select few, and is not publicly shared. Explicit knowledge is knowledge that is spoken aloud in order to teach or instruct others. It is publicly shared and is intended to be disseminated to other learners through broad diffusion or enhanced diffusion.

    c. Implicit knowledge is not conscious but intuitive; as it is readily accessible, it is important for full fluency. Explicit knowledge is conscious and reasoned, accessible through intentional, controlled processing and applied to resolve second language problems.

    d. Implicit knowledge is ambiguous; explicit knowledge is definitive.

25. Examples of non-Roman alphabetic languages include

    a. Sanskrit, Chinese, Arabic, Portuguese

    b. Senegalese, French, Arabic, Portuguese

    c. Chinese, Japanese, Arabic, Portuguese

    d. Chinese, Japanese, Arabic, Russian

26. What are contributing factors that influence a school district's choice of program models to best serve the needs of their student population?

    a. *b*, *c* and *d*

    b. available resources

    c. academic strength or weakness of English language learners

    d. needs of the community

27. Integrated content and learning instruction can best be described as
   a. teaching that combines L2 learning processes with curricular studies to the degree that each supports the other
   b. a focus on creating teaching models that conform to the curriculum and do not consider students' individual interests or abilities in order to produce a consistent set of expectations that can truly be assessed
   c. instruction that is based upon the accomplishment of real-world tasks, together with assessments that look at content areas for knowledge, skills and appropriate academic vocabulary
   d. a teaching model that integrates all members of the classroom, regardless of color, ethnicity or creed, and insuring that all members are content; learning takes place most readily when the students are comfortable within themselves and with one another

28. Words in two languages that are very similar in meaning and spelling, such as information/informacion, insect/insecto and comprehend/comprender, are called
   a. cognates
   b. hyperbole
   c. cognitive pairs
   d. idioms

29. A student is reading a picture book aloud. She reads one page slowly, working out the words she doesn't know with a variety of strategies including looking at the accompanying picture, recalling word-family relationships, and looking at the overall context. After she is confident she is reading the words correctly, she re-reads, picking up speed to make the sentences flow. She is enjoying her reading-aloud activity so much that she re-reads yet again, this time emphasizing important words with higher pitch or greater volume, and lowering her voice and slowing down to underscore dramatic moments. She is reading with
   a. comprehension, fluency and drama
   b. context, subtext and übertext
   c. context, smoothness and effect
   d. rate, accuracy and prosody

30. A fourth-grade teacher is explaining to her class that many words in English might have multiple meanings, depending upon content or context. She uses the word 'instruction' as an example, and asks her students to supply her with different uses. She begins by breaking the class into four heterogeneous groups and lets each group brainstorm. Next, the groups return to their seats and offer suggestions, which the teacher lists. Next to each definition, she writes 1, 2, 3 or 4 to correspond to the number of student groups that arrived at the same definition. The students are able to see that some definitions are more universally understood, such as 'teaching, lessons, set of steps, directions,' while others are more specific or obscure, such as 'guidance, tutoring' and 'advice.' Words that have multiple, sometimes unrelated meanings but retain a single spelling are called
    a. homogenic
    b. homophobic
    c. polysemous
    d. photogenic

31. Esteban's parents are fluent in both Spanish and English. They have heard about the one-parent, one-language approach, in which one parent exclusively uses Spanish and the other uses English. They believe this might resolve possible confusion for their son. This approach can lead to
    a. more rapid fluency in both English and Spanish
    b. psychological confusion and fears that one parent is preparing to leave
    c. passive bilingualism
    d. active monolingualism

32. In the integrated content and language instruction model, what is included in the category of academic language?
    a. Substantial non-social vocabulary, an understanding of Greek and Latin roots as well as a sufficient facility with Latinate prose styles
    b. Substantial antisocial vocabulary, including nonverbal communicatory skills such as facial expressions and body language
    c. Language that is highly abstract and theoretical with few concrete images or specific references; 'insider' language that intends to exclude nonmembers who lack understanding of the particular content area either through ignorance or lack of social standing
    d. Ideas and abstractions, essential vocabulary, specific grammatical uses and a familiarity with the discursive styles of various content areas

33. Cummin's Classification of Language and Content activities suggests a pair of continuums upon which learning can be based. One moves from information that is context-embedded to that which is context-minimized. The other begins with information that is cognitively undemanding and moves toward information that is cognitively demanding. According to his theory, lessons should begin at what point in both continuums?
    a. context-embedded and cognitively undemanding
    b. context-embedded and context minimized
    c. context-minimized and cognitively undemanding
    d. context-minimized and cognitively demanding

34. Most theorists agree that explicit knowledge plays a role in the attainment of a second language, but they disagree about the role. Which of the following best describes the function of explicit knowledge in the interface, weak interface and noninterface positions?
    a. In the noninterface position, explicit knowledge does not interfere with implicit knowledge and can, in fact, distract from it. From the weak interface position, explicit knowledge interferes only at the outset, after which implicit knowledge takes over and becomes primary. The interface position finds considerable interference unless the learner becomes hyper-alert to it and suppresses it in favor of implicit knowledge.
    b. In the noninterface position, explicit knowledge is completely unconnected to implicit knowledge and never transforms into it. From the weak interface position, explicit knowledge is useful in that it supports attention to the rules in the language during learning, which expedites the blossoming of implicit knowledge. The interface position finds learners with considerable occasions to practice speaking can transform explicit into implicit, unconscious knowledge.
    c. In the noninterface position, explicit knowledge is absent except to the degree a learner separates it from the vast, undifferentiated source. From the weak interface position, explicit knowledge rises on its own accord periodically, and it cannot be harnessed but does ultimately contribute to implicit knowledge. With the interface position, learners do not become fully fluent until they are able to slip from conscious use to unconscious use at will.
    d. In the noninterface position, explicit knowledge is the sole knowledge an unsophisticated speaker can use to become fluent. The weak interface position describes explicit knowledge as primarily important but not supremely so, in that learners can learn even when they aren't aware of it. However, this 'learning' is useless until the learner recognizes it and learns to manipulate it. The interface position finds that implicit knowledge must ultimately transform into explicit knowledge before a speaker is truly fluent.

35. This questionnaire regarding linguistic background must be filled in by the parent(s) or guardians of every LEP and kept in the student's record.
    a. Country of Origin Language Survey (COLS)
    b. Student Language History (SLH)
    c. Home Language Survey (HLS)
    d. History of Language Studies (HLS)

36. Transitional bilingual programs are those in which
    a. ELLs are transitioned, or exited, from the program into English-only classrooms within three months
    b. bilingual programs are extremely brief in nature (typically no more than three weeks), in which new ELLs are observed to determine which type of ESL or bilingual program will best serve them
    c. instruction is given in L1 and L2 so that the L1 is used in the service of L2s, putting it in a secondary position
    d. all bilingual and ESL programs are considered transitional, because the ultimate goal is a transition from L1 to L2 for primary language use

37. A first-grade class is creating a set of rules that will help them stay organized, straighten out problems between students and remain safe. This is an element of which first-grade curriculum?
    a. social studies
    b. health
    c. science
    d. none; it is simply common sense

38. A teacher knows her students are comfortable with addition, but only a few understand the concept of multiplication. She has decided it's time to make the leap. First, she demonstrates repeated addition: 3+3=6+3=9. She asks how many _times_ must 3 be added to something to get 9, then tells the students that 3 _times_ 3=9. Next, she gives them manipulatives containing nine identical items that are arranged into three distinct groups, and points out the relationship. After that, she asks for nine volunteers and arranges them into groups of three and has a volunteer first add the groups together, then multiply the groups. She shuffles the children around from group to group, so that the students are aware that similar items are counted in the same way, regardless of unique characteristics. Within a short period of time, while not all of her students can successfully multiply single-digits, all understand and can explain the concept of multiplication. Her methods are
    a. context analysis
    b. context assessment
    c. cognitive accountability
    d. comprehensive input

39. Define rubrics.
   a. a sheltered-English application
   b. a type of formative assessment
   c. a linguistically unique area in Ukraine
   d. a type of dictogloss

40. Hernando moved to the United States from Columbia four years ago. He has returned home three times. Before leaving the U.S., he became very anxious, repeatedly questioning his parents about his family members and Columbian culture. He was delighted, however, upon arrival, both at the attention he received and at the surprising familiarity of many aspects of the culture. However, certain things, such as the marketplace, confused him and made him uneasy. Still, he willingly went along with his grandmother, although as time went on she noticed he asked fewer and fewer questions and seemed less interested in the items for sale. She assumed this was because he had become used to the marketplace. When it was time to return to the U.S., Hernando exhibited the same anxiety as previously, and his parents noted that upon arrival, he was almost dazed by the speed at which people and machines moved. Hernando was demonstrating
   a. affective filter
   b. common childhood insecurity
   c. linguistic confusion
   d. culture shock cycle

41. What is required for re-designation?
   a. teacher reference; LAS or other oral fluency assessment; LAS or other reading/writing assessment; a writing sample; CTBS score in reading, language and math that is equal to or greater than 36%
   b. parent request; LAS or other oral fluency assessment; LAS or other reading/writing assessment; a writing sample; CTBS score in reading, language and math that is equal to or greater than 36%
   c. administrative request; LAS or other oral fluency assessment; a writing sample; CTBS score in reading, language and math that is equal to or greater than 73%
   d. LAS or other oral fluency assessment; LAS or other reading/writing assessment; a writing sample; CTBS score in reading, language and math that is equal to or greater than 69%

42. How has LEP enrollment changed in the school year 2005–2006 as compared to 2004–2005?
   a. It has nearly doubled, from 483,547 LEP learners to 896,435 learners.
   b. It has remained about the same.
   c. It has dropped by 32% from the previous year.
   d. It has dropped from approximately 684,000 to 641,000 learners.

43. Active student participation, social interaction, integrated oral and written language, authentic books and tasks and adequate coverage of background knowledge are key components of what type of program?
   a. English as a second language (ESL)
   b. specially designated academic instruction in English (SDAIE)
   c. two-way immersion (TWI)
   d. my-way immersion (MWI)

44. A dictogloss is
   a. a task in which students take dictation as a native speaker reads a paragraph aloud, compare their scripted paragraphs to one another's, then compare them to the original text.
   b. a task in which students listen to a brief content-based lecture for main idea, then for details, recreate the lecture independently, consider each version as a group and select the most accurate.
   c. a task in which students dictate a memory, personal experience or other privately-owned perception to a bilingual partner; the partner writes down the dictation in her L1; the same partner then translates the dictation into English and has the native speaker correct her errors.

45. LAS, BINL, PT, QSE and WML are all examples of
   a. CVC words
   b. phonemic arrangements not permitted in English
   c. language assessments
   d. nonsense; there are no such acronyms

46. Much has been written about the importance of context in communication. A group of speakers at a café is highly likely to refer to events, people or objects outside the window or behind the counter without naming them or even indicating them linguistically. For example, two young girls might see a boy they find attractive and giggle, as one of them utters, 'cute!' The study of context in communication is called
   a. context
   b. subtext
   c. externals
   d. pragmatics

47. The second most extensively utilized alphabetic system in the world is the _____ alphabet.
   a. Roman
   b. Greek
   c. Chinese
   d. Arabic

48. When must every LEP be assessed for primary language proficiency?
    a. no later than 30 calendar days after enrollment
    b. no later than 10 calendar days after enrollment
    c. no later than 45 calendar days after enrollment
    d. no later than 90 calendar days after enrollment

49. Historically, what theoretical position resulted in the integrated content and language instruction model, and when?
    a. in the early 1970s, from research indicating that L2 learning is expedited when content is the instructional focus rather than a separate content area focused purely on language learning
    b. in the late 1950s, from the hypothesis that knowledge from all content areas all ultimately sources back to a kind of Ur-knowledge, including languages, practical knowledge, personal knowledge and academic knowledge
    c. This position is new and currently evolving, and offers a fabric woven from numerous theoretical and pragmatic beliefs too numerous to mention.
    d. There is no such instructional model.

50. LAS stands for
    a. Language Assessment Standards
    b. Linguistic Achievement Score
    c. Language Assessment Scales
    d. Learning Attitude Studies

51. The audio-lingual approach to language acquisition relies upon
    a. manipulatives, diagrams, charts and other visual aids and physical involvement with projects
    b. listening, speaking, reading, writing
    c. drilling, imitating and pantomime
    d. pairing students heterogeneously

52. Dr. Yang's bilingual students have just completed producing a class newspaper. They interviewed other students, wrote editorials, created a page of ads, reviewed several lunch offerings, and created both a cartoon page and a horoscope section. Last month the students wrote a brochure for a mythical video games company. Next month, the students will each do an oral presentation on a topic of their own choosing. At the end of the semester, the entire class will perform a play they have written, cast and directed on their own. What type of learning is this teacher involving her students in?
    a. high motivation learning
    b. pleasure-based learning
    c. learning through the use of manipulatives
    d. task-based learning

53. As a result of Lau v. Nichols, the Department of Health, Education and Welfare established procedures to help districts with LEP students create programs to accommodate their needs. What administration discontinued these guidelines?
   a. Nixon Administration
   b. Kennedy Administration
   c. Reagan Administration
   d. Bush Administration

54. English contains thousands of allowable syllables, while a language such as Japanese contains approximately 100. What accounts for this?
   a. English is far more expressive than Japanese.
   b. English is based on the Roman alphabet; Japanese is based on Chinese.
   c. English is based on the Roman alphabet; Japanese is idiographic.
   d. English has more vowels than many other languages, and a high number of consonant clusters.

55. Ms. McGravada uses sheltered English strategies with her students. She believes that ideas and broad concepts are the base upon which literacy is built. During a typical day, which of the following is she likely to employ?
   a. drilling word-families, irregular verbs, spelling, and math
   b. offering pieces of essential knowledge repeatedly, using a variety of strategies, and checking periodically to make sure students understand
   c. using manipulatives and visual aids such as graphs, diagrams, and charts
   d. b and c

56. One way a norm-referenced assessment arrives at a student's scores is by comparing the student with others who have achieved the same score in relative terms of their ages. The average age of people who received the same score as the individual child. The results will indicate the child is at the same level as other learners her age, is at the same level as younger learners, or the same level as older learners. This is called a(n)
   a. grade placement score
   b. age-adjusted score
   c. age-equivalent score
   d. norm-converted score

57. Programs such as language immersion, sheltered English, content instruction in English, English as a second language and other successful programs share what essential characteristics?

    a. comprehending the needs and prior knowledge of their ELLs, designing instruction accordingly, assessing and adjusting instruction as needed

    b. designing research projects that involve their ELLs, designing instruction accordingly, assessing instruction to determine the most successful methods

    c. assessing individual students upon enrollment, blending tried-and-true methods with innovative approaches, working with home families

    d. assessing families to determine level of first language development, enriching both first and second language academic and social development, recording and reporting results

58. The Bilingual Education Acts of 1968 and 1974 supplied additional monies for districts to create programs for ELL students and are also known as

    a. Title VI

    b. Title VII

    c. the Doubletalk Act

    d. Into the Future VII

59. Formative assessments include

    a. final examinations, state and national tests, college-entrance exams

    b. formal assessments, standardized tests, college-entrance exams

    c. on-going assessments, informal observations, quizzes, diagnostic tests

    d. quarterly assessments, informal quizzes, pre-enrollment assessments

60. An ELL's parents have concerns that their daughter is confused in her bilingual classroom. They think it might be best for her to be in an English-only classroom in order to develop her listening, speaking and reading skills. Neither parent is English-fluent, but they recognize that their child frequently combines Spanish and English in the same sentence. The teacher has noticed that the child 'mixes up' the two languages. What is the best course of action?

    a. Immediately enroll her in a pull-out immersion class.

    b. Leave her where she is, but observe her carefully for signs of learning disabilities.

    c. Leave her where she is, but pull her out for part of each day for ESL instruction.

    d. Leave her where she is; monitor her and adjust instruction accordingly.

61. In Texas, balanced language two-way immersion programs are _____ minority-language dominant programs.

    a. equivalent to

    b. significantly greater than

    c. significantly less than

    d. nearly the same as

62. The Center for Research on Education, Diversity & Excellence (CREDE) holds the position that ELLs succeed best when
    a. participating in a language submersion program in which academic instruction is in their first language and supported in their second language
    b. receiving academic instruction in their first language as well as instruction in English throughout the day
    c. participating in a language submersion program in which academic instruction is in their second language and supported in their first language
    d. participating in a language submersion program in which academic instruction is in their first language and supported in their first and second languages

63. What governing body is accountable for overseeing programs for Limited English Proficiency students?
    a. the school district
    b. the Federal Department of Education
    c. the State Department of Education
    d. the county

64. What are some types of authentic assessments?
    a. informal assessment, formal assessment and self-assessment
    b. psychological assessment, outcomes assessment and portfolios
    c. performance assessment, portfolios and student self-assessment
    d. dialogue, written assessment and concept analysis assessment

65. How many phonemes are represented by the 29 letters of the Spanish alphabet?
    a. 24
    b. 29
    c. 41
    d. 58

66. CALLA stands for
    a. Competency Assessment for Language Learners All
    b. Cognitive Academic Language Learning Approach
    c. Categories Arrangements for Laddered Linguistics Approaches
    d. a type of flower: CALLA is a kindergarten program in which students are represented as blossoming flowers in a kinder-'garden'

67. Numerous studies indicate that students in _____ programs are more academically successful than those in _____ programs, but not as successful as students in _____ and _____ programs.
    a. early exit; ESL, late exit; two-way bilingual
    b. ESL; early exit; late exit; two-way bilingual
    c. late exit; early exit; ESL; two-way bilingual
    d. ESL; two-way bilingual; early exit; late exit

68. BICS and CALP are both concerned with oral communication, but they each focus on different areas of communicative development. Of the following, which most accurately characterizes the two?

a. Best Instructional Conversational Skills and Conversations Among Language Practitioners exhibit no crossover. BICS is a highly idealized academic approach in which learners follow a strictly proscribed set of instructional steps, while BICS is pragmatically concerned with authentic dialogue that may be imperfectly rendered but is nonetheless highly meaningful to the speaker and, in the best case, to the listener as well.

b. Basic Instructional Concept Skills and Cognitive Academic Linguistic Pragmatics are primarily separate pursuits but do include some common ground. BICS is theory-based and teaches L2 learners concepts of education in American classrooms, such as research-read-analyze-write or learning to read/reading to learn. CALP instruction takes a pragmatic, hands-on approach in which mini-lessons are taught when they arise as questions in a student's learning.

c. Bilingual Independent Classroom Strategies and Classrooms for All Learning Processes share a greater degree of commonality. BICS encourages students to proceed with learning to the furthest degree they are able, asking for language support along the way. CALP students are also encouraged to work independently and at their own speeds, but since there are many learning styles, some students may request help, others may research it, and still others may attack it through creativity or analysis.

d. Basic Interpersonal Communicative Skills and Cognitive Academic Language Proficiency are concerned with entirely different types of communication. BICS is 'survival English,' requiring basic language skills for face-to-face communication that depends heavily upon the speakers' shared context and is typically arrived at within the first two years of exposure to English. CALP is a more specialized application of English, and requires on average five or more years for a student to gain academic proficiency appropriate to his grade level.

69. A teacher has a new student in her class from Norway. The student is fluent in English, but very shy. The teacher has brought several story books to class. She has a book written in Norwegian as well as folk and fairy tales that originated in Norway. She made the new student laugh by attempting to read the Norwegian book aloud. The student offered to read it for her, then taught her new classmates several words in her native language. The teacher has

a. lightened the student's cultural load
b. engaged the student using innovative techniques
c. lightened the student's linguistic load
d. introduced the student to American culture

70. Describe the difference between a morpheme and a phoneme.
    a. A phoneme is the smallest unit of distinctive sound; a morpheme is the smallest unit of distinctive meaning.
    b. A morpheme is the smallest unit of distinctive sound; a morpheme is the smallest unit of distinctive meaning.
    c. They are interchangeable.
    d. A morpheme is a phoneme that has 'morphed,' or gained subtextual meaning.

71. When an L2 becomes self-conscious or insecure around other students, she might develop negative perceptions that discourage her willingness to take the risks necessary for language-learning. These negative perceptions are grouped together and referred to as
    a. hypersensitivity
    b. affective filter
    c. effective filter
    d. defective filter

72. The Civil Rights Language Minority Regulations of 1980 set policy for the identification, assessment, services offered and exit strategies for bilingual students. What is one mandate of the Act?
    a. Qualified teachers must offer the bilingual instruction.
    b. All new students must be assessed.
    c. Once entered into a bilingual program, students must remain for at least four years.
    d. English instruction must be offered to the student's family as well as to the student.

73. How many years of combined quality instruction in both first and second languages does research indicate is needed in order for bilingual students to succeed to the same degree as native English speakers?
    a. three to four years
    b. Research indicates that no amount of combined instruction can bring a bilingual student to the level of academic success as a native English speaker.
    c. seven years or more
    d. four to seven years

74. A teaching program is designed to simultaneously teach L1 and L2 students equally by offering content instruction in both languages. L2 learners gain facility with English as well as the content areas, while L1 learners gain facility with a second language as well as the content areas. Biliteracy, academic achievement and appreciation of both cultures are the goals of such instruction. This approach is called
    a. bilateral learning
    b. bicultural education
    c. two-way immersion
    d. secondary submersion

75. A late-exit bilingual program serves students in grades _____, and provides students with a minimum of _____ of their class time with teaching in their L1.
 a. K–1st; 40%
 b. K–12; 50%
 c. K–4; 60%
 d. K–6; 40%

76. A fourth-grade teacher is preparing her students for a geography lesson. She lists the following words on the board and discusses their meanings: *Latitude, longitude, grid, absolute, relative.* She points out that some of the words have common meanings as well as meanings specific to geography. These content-specific words are
 a. tier 1 words
 b. tier 2 words
 c. tier 3 words
 d. tier 4 words

77. Language Proficiency Assessment committees have a number of possible tasks. They are required to fulfill a minimum of two designated tasks per student. These tasks include determining the proficiency level for all LEPs, determining the level of academic achievement, supporting an LEP's involvement in other programs and
 a. classifying appropriate LEPs as proficient and recommending program exit
 b. providing extracurricular support for LEPs and their families through tutoring, community activities and other opportunities
 c. selecting suitable methods of assessment for each student prior to the annual state criterion referenced test
 d. *a* and *c*

78. Bilingual education has been a point of conflict for several decades. Common arguments opposing such education include the concern that students whose first language is not English will be discouraged from learning English if presented with an easier option, that it interferes with cultural integration and
 a. that it is too expensive
 b. that it negatively affects the quality of instruction native speakers receive
 c. that it results in delayed L2 development, rather than supporting it
 d. all the above

79. Summative assessments include
 a. final examinations, state and national tests, college-entrance exams
 b. formal assessments, standardized tests, college-entrance exams
 c. on-going assessments, informal observations, quizzes, diagnostic tests
 d. quarterly assessments, informal quizzes, pre-enrollment assessments

80. The Bilingual Education and Training Act of 1973 required that elementary public schools in Texas with at least _____ LEP students at a grade level make bilingual teaching available.
  a. 40
  b. 60
  c. 5
  d. 20

81. Pre-departure and resettlement Cultural Orientation programs were developed
  a. in the mid-70s, when South Vietnam, Laos and Cambodian governments were in crisis and hundreds of thousands of refugees fled
  b. in 1993, when many Americans began to emigrate to Asia, Australia and Europe
  c. following WWII, when Japanese nationals were released from internment camps
  d. in the late 1980s, when the worldwide economic downturn resulted in many illegal immigrants crossing the border from Mexico

82. Data gathered by the Center for Applied Linguistics indicates that more than half of minority-language and less than half of majority-language students receive reduced-price or free lunches. This information is
  a. false
  b. neither true nor false; such information has not been gathered
  c. neither true nor false; gathering such information would be a civil rights violation
  d. true

83. Krashen's model of Input+1 describes
  a. the importance of pairing students homogeneously
  b. the importance of pairing students heterogeneously
  c. the idea that new knowledge should be offered at a level just slightly above the learner's current knowledge
  d. the idea that new, scaffolded knowledge must 'rest' for one day before being referred to or recalled

84. As a result of Lau v. Nichols (U.S. Supreme Court, 1974) L2 learners must
  a. be given the same educational opportunities as L1 learners.
  b. be given instruction they are capable of understanding.
  c. be held back until they master grade-level material in English.
  d. be assessed frequently, with teaching adjusted accordingly.

85. When a dominant culture absorbs and transforms members of a minority culture, it is _____. When a dominant culture transforms and is transformed by members of a minority culture, it is _____.
    a. acculturation; acquisition
    b. acculturation; assimilation
    c. assimilation; acquisition
    d. assimilation; acculturation

86. A second-grade teacher is preparing an integrated content and language lesson on types of homes mammals construct. Which of the following sets might she write in order to clarify outcome expectations for both herself and her students?
    a. Students will learn to identify types of mammal homes by name (burrow, nest, den, lair, lodge, etc.). Students will be able to discuss where these homes can be found. Students will be able to speculate about how these homes are constructed through drawing, writing, charting or graphically organizing their ideas.
    b. Students will learn about animal homes. Students will discuss animal homes and what they are used for. Students will write a funny story about an animal who cannot find his home and 'tries on' the homes of several other animals before he is rescued by a kindly old owl.
    c. Students will read about mammal homes. Students will write about mammal homes, bird homes and human homes. Students will enjoy this lesson.
    d. Students will compare and contrast human and mammalian homes using a variety of texts and diagrams, working first singly and later in L1-L2 pairs. They will then articulate the results of this research in a classroom presentation. Finally, the entire class will create a statistical analysis of how many class members have had direct experience with one or more of these mammal structures.

87. A fourth-grade teacher has given a writing assignment. Students are to write a 'portrait' in which they describe someone they have seen but do not know. They are asked to use vivid verbs that create an image, focus on small, telling details, use correct punctuation, capitalize appropriately and write in the present tense. They are also asked to use adjectives that specify (such as 'lime-green' or 'murky') instead of those that exaggerate or dramatize without adding real information (such as 'enormous' or 'beautiful'). The students will create a first draft. Next, they will be paired with another student, and each student will be given the following chart, which has been printed on both sides of a page:

	Unclear or insufficient	Sufficient	Exceptional
Vivid verbs			
Specific details			
Correct punctuation			
Capitalization			
Present tense throughout			

Each student will review first his own work, then his partner's. This type of assessment is called
    a. shared learning
    b. shared assessment
    c. shared clarification
    d. rubrics

88. Communicative approaches to instruction where learning is a collaboration between the teacher and students. The teacher acts primarily as a catalyst, and works alongside students to decide upon curriculum content and systematize the ways in which it will be taught. Examples of this approach include
    a. Enlightened Eclecticism, Total Physical Response
    b. Humanistic Approach, Silent Way
    c. Natural Approach, Suggestopedia
    d. all the above

89. A teacher has a student from Japan who cannot pronounce /l/ or /r/, but rather blends the two. While he recognizes the differences between words such as 'light' and 'right' in reading, if they are spoken, especially within the context of a sentence, he cannot differentiate. She also has several children from Mexico who have similar problems with /b/ and /v/. Why is this?
    a. These sounds are not represented in their L1 alphabets, and so are 'invisible.'
    b. These sounds are not distinct in their L1 phonemes, and so are 'invisible.'
    c. These sounds are not 'invisible,' since the children recognize their distinctiveness in   reading. The students should be seen by a speech therapist, as the problem might be physical.
    d. Because these students are new to the U.S., they are no doubt experiencing culture shock. They are overwhelmed by new information on a daily basis, and gravitate toward those elements that are most familiar.

90. PEPSI is
    a. stages of language development
    b. a soft drink
    c. Periodic Evaluative Proficient Student Index
    d. Prevalent-Equivalent Projects in Social Inequity

91. A building with a minimum of 21 LEP students must provide a committee made up of teachers, other school employees who serve the students and
    a. the student
    b. parents
    c. volunteer professionals within the community
    d. paid professionals within the community

92. Title VII, the Bilingual Language Act, requires that districts whose student population contains over 5% who have a nation of origin other than the U.S. provide second-language instruction for those students. This act also forbids placing LEP students in handicapped or vocational classes based on lack of language proficiency only, as well as requiring
    a. a pull-out program for LEPs at least twice a week
    b. a free-lunch program for immigrant students, regardless of economic need
    c. assessment of ELLs from enrollment through exit
    d. communication between parents and school administrators in a language parents can understand

93. Summarizing, question generating, clarifying and predicting are used in what teaching method?
    a. sheltered English
    b. reciprocal teaching
    c. spontaneous combustion
    d. simultaneous teaching

94. How long does it take CALP skills to develop?
    a. 3 years or more
    b. 4 years or more
    c. 5 years or more
    d. 7 years or more

95. Which type of content-based work is most productive in supporting second-language acquisition?
    a. work that requires students to recall academic language and generate written or spoken discourse that depends upon it
    b. work that requires students to listen and repeat
    c. work that requires students to research new academic language and integrate it into dialogue
    d. work that requires students to listen and respond

- 112 -

96. Two commercially produced assessment tools focus on oral grammar: the Basic Inventory of Natural Language (BINL) and
    a. the Bilingual Syntax Measure (BSM)
    b. the Oral Competency Assessment (OCA)
    c. the Listening and Speaking Skills Scales (LSSS)
    d. the Dialogue Charts (DC)

97. The Additive Model of language acquisition, also known as the Common Underlying Proficiency Model, finds that sufficient exposure to two languages promotes the underlying linguistic development in both. The opposing model is
    a. Disparate Underlying Proficiency model
    b. Anti-CUP
    c. SUP
    d. Subtractive Model

98. The three types of language writing systems are alphabetic, _____ and
    _____
    a. syllabic; logographic
    b. syllabic; ideological
    c. logographic; ideological
    d. syllabic; largographic

99. A task-based approach to teaching focuses on
    a. specific language learning 'tasks' such as learning adjectives, subject-verb agreement rules, or memorizing verb conjugations
    b. a series of tasks the teacher must perform in rigorous order
    c. a series of seemingly overwhelming tasks, such as those given fairy tale heroes, for the learner to accomplish and resolve learning whatever language skills she possesses; for example, a student is instructed to go to a mall alone and to intentionally become lost, ask for directions or help, and return home completely on her own
    d. using language as a medium for the message, rather than making the memorizing of its rules an end in itself

100. Language Acquisition Theory finds distinct areas of development for acquiring a language and learning about a language. _____ is _____ a language, while _____ is a(n)_____ process when language is used in authentic communication.
    a. Knowledge; learning about; acquisition; conscious
    b. Learning; knowing about; acquisition; unconscious
    c. Learning; knowing about; consciousness; acquired
    d. Learning; knowing about; unconsciousness; acquired

Answers and Explanations

1. B: formulaic expressions; rules of the language. Research indicates that early second-language learners absorb a few formulaic expressions and initially do not perceive them as separate words so much as functional phrases that are memorized as global wholes. Phrases such as "I don't want to go" or "Where is the grocery store" later become templates for discovering the rules of the language. "I don't want to go" becomes the formula for "I don't like my neighbor" or "I don't understand"; with time, the learner understands the subject can change, and that the verb must change in agreement. "I don't want to go" becomes a template for "Paula wants a dog" or "My friend doesn't like shopping."

2. B: static, with fewer than a dozen documented programs. While currently there are 248 programs nationwide, the majority of these were established in the last 20 years. In the two decades following the development of the first TWI program, growth was extremely slow, with fewer than a dozen programs prior to the 1980s.

3. D: information-gap tasks. This strategy involves pairing students, who are given two very similar texts that differ in key points. They must read and compare, then determine which portion of which text is accurate based upon textual context, their combined prior knowledge and logical guesses. Finally, the pair must create a new version in which the accurate information in the two texts is melded.

4. C: the Civil Rights Act. The Civil Rights Act of 1964, or Title VI, abolishes discrimination in programs that receive federal funding. In essence, the Act establishes that all students have the right to the same high quality of instruction.

5. C: Yes, as long as she's lived outside the U.S. for at least two full years. She lived in Mexico for the first four years of her life, so she meets the requirements.

6. B: BICS. Basic Interpersonal Communication Skills (BICS) include vocabulary, syntax and style used in daily informal activities that don't require a great deal of thought. Ideas that rely upon BICS to be communicated are typically concrete, immediate, known or familiar rather than abstract, unknown or mysterious. BICS typically develop within the first 2–3 years of first exposure. Sufficient facility with BICS should not be the sole criterion for putting a student into a learning environment where L2 is the only language used in instruction.

7. C: Her fears, while understandable, are not supported by research. In fact, students in bilingual classrooms achieve linguistic facility at about the same rate, and have advantages in terms of more specialized knowledge in some areas.

8. B: RPTE. Reading Proficiency Tests in English. RPTE, together with the Texas Observation Protocols (TOPS), compose the Texas English Language Proficiency System (TELPAS).

9. C: meaning, because ELLs are better able to decode messages and encode their own ideas when they are motivated by the desire and actively attempting to communicate something meaningful.

10. C: English as a second language. English as a second language programs do not necessarily use students' L1s in instruction. ESL programs differ from other bilingual programs in that English submersion in the classroom is emphasized and pull-out time is used remedially.

11. B: National Clearinghouse for English Language Acquisition; "To collect, coordinate and convey a broad range of research and resources in support of an inclusive approach to high quality education for ELLs."

12. A: one in which the minority language is employed instructionally at least 80% of the time. A minority language two-way immersion program focuses on the L2 for teaching 80% of the time or more.

13. D: There are planned outcomes for both content and language learning; goal-oriented interaction takes place; tasks that advance listening, speaking, reading and writing are integrated; outcomes are continuously observed and assessed. Integrated content and language instruction is supported with focused and directed tasks from start to finish.

14. B: slipping back and forth between two languages. When a bilingual speaker slips back and forth between two languages, it causes some observers to be concerned that the speaker is confused. Actually, research indicates comfortably moving between languages, even in the same oral statement, suggests competency with both languages.

15. B: No, spelling and pronunciation are not perfectly aligned. While anticipating correct pronunciation from a written word in Spanish is generally easy, an orally produced word is not necessarily as transparent in terms of the letters conventionally used to script it. Each alphabetic letter in Spanish is associated with only one phoneme; however, some phonemes have more than one letter to represent them.

16. B: Each lesson is designed to result in specific content and language learning goals. Lessons encourage students to communicate with other members of the classroom and the teacher in order to achieve specific skills and understanding related to the content. The teacher offers tasks that encourage all language skills— listening, speaking, writing, and reading within content areas. Ongoing results within the learning process are noted and assessed as part of the lesson.

17. C: educating immigrants in terms of cultural mores, necessary skills and knowledge. Cultural Orientation offers refugees and other immigrants language training that is geared to be practical rather than comprehensive; language skills focus on real-life situations such as following directions, reading instructions or communicating with a doctor. Immigrants are taught how to read subway maps, obey traffic rules and behave in ways that are socially acceptable in the United States.

18. D: story retelling. Sections of the LAS include recognition of sounds/phrases; the ability to reproduce the same; vocabulary; comprehension; and story-retelling, the last of which is 50% of the total score.

19. B: ESL students lose facility with their original language, while those in TWI programs don't lose facility while learning English.

20. A: For each year, each state is required to report increases in the percentage of students making progress in learning English; increases in percentage of students achieving English proficiency; ELL students making Adequate Yearly Progress.

21. B: improve teaching methods. Formative assessments such as observational notes, quizzes, tests and writing, and diagnostic tests are methods of ongoing assessment that are used to fine-tune, redesign or streamline teaching strategies.

22. B: listening, speaking, reading and writing. These are the four ways in which language is used, and each has some unique characteristics.

23. A: Clarify her goals by writing them down, using descriptive verbs such as 'discuss, listen, ask, point out' and 'demonstrate.' Clarifying her goals by mindfully selecting precise verbs helps Ms. Hernandez understand the similar and different requirements of the language component and content component of her lesson. Additionally, by sharing her written goals with her students and reviewing them during the lesson, class members develop a heightened awareness of the shared but unique goals.

24. C: Implicit knowledge is not conscious but intuitive; as it is readily accessible, it is important for full fluency. Explicit knowledge is conscious and reasoned, accessible through intentional, controlled processing and applied to resolve second language problems.

25. D: Chinese, Japanese, Arabic, Russian for the correct response. Chinese is ideographic at its roots; while it is incorrect to say that all Chinese characters are pictographs, many currently are while others originated in a pictograph that has, over time, become increasingly abstract. Moreover, each character in written in Chinese represents an entire word, not a phonemic or syllabic unit. There are over 40,000 Chinese characters, although most users know, at most, around 5,000.

Japanese, which is composed of approximately 100 distinct morphemes, uses a syllabic writing system in which each character represents a complete sound group, rather than an individual phoneme, as in English. To the uninitiated, Japanese and Chinese can appear identical; in reality, the Japanese written form borrowed ideographs from Chinese and re-assigned them syllabic 'meanings.' The Arabic alphabet is close to the top of the most widely used alphabets world-wide, currently used by over 100 languages, including Persian, Kurdish, and Urdu. Its roots are in the Phoenician alphabet; there is no distinction made between upper and lower case letters and there are no written representations for vowels. The Russian alphabet is Cyrillic and is rooted in Greek. Composed of 33 letters, it is used to script well over 50 languages, including Serbian, Bulgarian, Ukrainian and Mongolian.

26. A: *b*, *c* and *d*. A district will choose from available program models for bilingual/ESL education based upon a number of variables, including available resources, availability of fluently bilingual teachers, the academic abilities of students, the needs of the community and the ideologies of the programs under consideration.

27. C: instruction that is based upon the accomplishment of real-world tasks, together with assessments that look at content areas for knowledge, skills and appropriate academic vocabulary. Integrated content and learning instruction finds instructional and learning value in the practice of skills and knowledge students are likely to encounter in their experiences.

28. A: cognates. Cognates are word-pairs in which the words belong to two different languages but are clearly related both in terms of spelling and in terms of meaning.

29. D: rate, accuracy and prosody. The student begins by working on her accuracy, so that when she picks up speed she will neither mistake one word for another, nor mispronounce a word. Next, she re-reads at a steady, smooth rate. Finally, she reads by grouping certain phrases and underscoring certain words to achieve a dramatic affect; this is known as prosody.

30. C: polysemous. Polysemous words have a variety of meanings, and depend upon context or content to determine which meaning is valid. They are typically words that are used in a specific situation or content area, and often also have informal or social applications.

31. C: passive bilingualism. The one-parent, one-language approach sometimes does result in a child's fluency in both languages. However, this outcome is not guaranteed. Depending upon other factors such as social context, the child's learning style, motivation and emotive sensibilities, this approach can also result in a child who understands both languages but is reluctant to express herself or her ideas in either.

32. D: ideas and abstractions, essential vocabulary, specific grammatical uses and a familiarity with the discursive styles of various content areas. Academic language is imbued with formality. It tends toward words with Latin or Greek roots, expresses concepts, ideas and abstractions, utilizes vocabulary specific to the content area, and may use individualized and even idiosyncratic grammar.

33. A: context-embedded and cognitively undemanding. Context-embedded instruction is less abstract and easier to understand because it is less language-dependent than context-minimized instruction. Cognitively undemanding instruction will be easily understood and followed by learners. Therefore, according to Cummins, lessons should begin at these points in their respective continuums.

34. B: In the noninterface position, explicit knowledge is completely unconnected to implicit knowledge and never transforms into it. From the weak interface position, explicit knowledge is useful in that it supports attention to the rules in the language during learning, which expedites the blossoming of implicit knowledge. The interface position finds learners with considerable occasions to practice speaking can transform explicit into implicit, unconscious knowledge.

35. C: Home Language Survey. This survey is a form that must be filled in by a parent or guardian of an LEP student, providing information about that student's history in terms of his language development, exposure and experiences.

36. C: instruction is given in L1 and L2 so that the L1 is used in the service of L2s, putting it in a secondary position. Transitional bilingual programs depend upon instruction given in both L1 and L2, but numerous studies have described the L1 use as being secondary. The goal of these programs is that students be early-or-late-exit transitioned (depending upon the program) into an English-only classroom.

37. A: social studies. First grade social studies curriculum focuses on familial, peer, classroom and community relationships; multicultural traditions and holidays; why rules and laws are necessary and how they are used.

38. D: comprehensive input. Input+1 is instruction within reach, that is implanted in a context that is significant to the learner, modified (simplified, repeated, re-worded), involves collaboration and is explored through a variety of modalities.

39. B: a type of formative assessment. Formative assessments are on-going, and used to fine-tune instruction or learning. Rubrics can be used to assess a student or peer, and it is also commonly used for self-assessment.

40. D: culture shock cycle, is also referred to as cultural adaptation. There are a number of distinct phases including nervousness before departure, early contentment upon arrival; culture shock; apparent social adjustment that is not deeply rooted; mental loneliness; nervousness about returning; culture shock.

41. A: teacher reference; LAS or other oral fluency assessment; LAS or other reading/writing assessment; a writing sample; a California Test of Basic Skills (CTBS) score in reading, language and math that is equal to or greater than 36%.

42. D: It has dropped from approximately 684,000 to 641,000 learners. According to data collected and analyzed by the National Clearinghouse, total student enrollment for the state of Texas in 2005–2006 was 4,525,394, which represents a 13.6% growth over total enrollment 1995–1996, the first year in which the data was collected. LEP enrollment in 2005–2006 was 640,749, a 34% increase in LEP growth since 1995–1996. Total LEP enrollment the previous year (2004–2005) was 684,007, a 43% growth over LEP enrollment in 1995–1996.

43. B: specially designated academic instruction in English (SDAIE). SDAIE is content and subject area instruction that serves the needs of ELLs by encouraging active participation, social connection, the integration of written and spoken language, books and tasks that are relevant to the learners, and support in terms of background knowledge.

44. B: a task in which students listen to a brief content-based lecture for main idea, then for details, recreate the lecture independently, consider each version as a group and select the most accurate.

45. C: language assessments. Language Assessment Scores (LAS), Basic Inventory of Natural Language (BINL), Ideal Oral Proficiency (PT), Quick Start in English (QSE) and the Woodcock-Munoz Language Survey (WML) are used to assess students' fluency with language.

46. D: pragmatics. Pragmatics studies how context provides extra-linguistic information that enriches and shapes oral communication.

47. D: Arabic. Written Arabic contains 28 letters, and makes no distinction between upper and lower cases. When printed or written, letters attach to one another, changing their appearances dependent upon which letters they are next to. Vowels have no written expression in Arabic, the second-most-used alphabetic system in the world.

48. D: no later than 90 calendar days after enrollment. LEPS must be assessed for primary language proficiency within the first three months of their enrollment.

49. A: in the early 1970s, from research indicating that L2 learning is expedited when content is the instructional focus rather than a separate content area focused purely on language learning.

50. C: Language Assessment Scales. The LAS is available in Spanish, Vietnamese, Tagalalog and Apache as well as in English. Sections of the LAS include recognition

of sounds/phrases, the ability to reproduce the same, vocabulary, comprehension and story-retelling.

51. C: drilling, imitation and mime. The audio-lingual approach is a non-communicative position that relies upon repetition, drill and imitation. It is not effective.

52. D: task-based learning. Task-based learning explores the many uses of language through 'tasks' or activities that require specific uses, vocabulary and styles rather than through a syntactical structure, a group of vocabulary words, or word families to teach a second language. Tasks are seen as fundamental to learning because learners are attending to the task instead of concerned with their language use. When the task has been completed, the teacher uses it to demonstrate areas of linguistic misunderstanding and corrections.

53. C: Reagan Administration. As a result of Lau v. Nichols, HEW offered specific procedures to be used with LEP students. The Reagan Administration discontinued the guidelines.

54. D: English has more vowels than many other languages, and a high number of consonant clusters. Japanese is a syllabically represented language in written form; the entire language is composed of approximately 100 syllables, which means many words must be multisyllabic. Such written styles are not used for languages with large numbers of syllabic possibilities, such as English, which contains thousands of allowable syllables because of the number of vowels, the multiple ways in which vowels can be pronounced, and the large number of consonant clusters.

55. D: *b* and *c*. Some of the methods used in sheltered English are repeating pieces of essential knowledge, using a variety of strategies, checking periodically to make sure students understand and using manipulatives and visual aids such as graphs, diagrams and charts.

56. C: age-equivalent score. One way a norm-referenced assessment arrives at a student's scores is by comparing the student with others who have achieved the same score in relative terms of their ages. The average age of people who received the same score as the individual child. The results will indicate the child is at the same level as other learners her age, is at the same level as younger learners, or the same level as older learners.

57. A: comprehending the needs and prior knowledge of their ELLs, designing instruction accordingly, assessing and adjusting instruction as needed.

58. B: Title VII. The Bilingual Education Acts of 1968 and 1974 provide monies to districts to establish programs for the special needs of ELLs.

59. C: on-going assessments, informal observations, quizzes, diagnostic tests. Formative assessments are used to monitor the effectiveness of instructional methods.

60. D: Leave her where she is; monitor her and adjust instruction accordingly. Evidence from numerous research studies indicates that using two languages simultaneously does not confuse the users.

61. D: nearly the same as. In Texas, there are only slightly more balanced language two-way immersion programs (47%) as there are minority-language dominant programs (41%).

62. B: receiving academic instruction in their first language as well as instruction in English throughout the day. According to CREDE, "English language learners (ELLs) also benefit from on-grade-level academic instruction in their first language. These benefits begin in the first years of schooling, and if such instruction is sustained, the benefits are cumulative. ELLs whose schooling develops them academically and cognitively, using their first language, are more successful in English-based instruction by the end of their school years than those ELL students who are not provided such first-language instruction."

63. C: the State Department of Education. Idaho v. Migrant Council (1981) determined the State Department of Education bears the legal responsibility of monitoring LEP programs.

64. C: performance assessment, portfolios and student self-assessment. Authentic assessment combines various evaluative tools to determine the degree of learning, success, motivation and attitudes a student brings to classroom learning.

65. A: 24. The Spanish alphabet, with 29 letters, is similar to the English alphabet, but it contains *ll, rr* and *ñ*. These letters represent 24 phonemes.

66. B: Cognitive Academic Language Learning Approach. CALLA approaches instruction with explicit teaching strategies divided into the categories of metacognitive, which refers to planning, self-observing, and being aware of the process; cognitive, or summarizing, deducing, considering ideas; and social-affective, which includes social activities such as asking and answering questions, peer evaluation and cooperative learning.

67. A: early exit; ESL; late exit; two-way bilingual. Early exit programs are less effective because exiting occurs before most students are ready (Collier, 1992). However, they are oftentimes more academically more successful than those in pull-out ESL programs. But programs in which students remain for several years (late-exit), as well as two-way programs, are both more successful.

68. D: Basic Interpersonal Communicative Skills and Cognitive Academic Language Proficiency are concerned with entirely different types of communication. BICS is 'survival English,' requiring basic language skills for face-to-face communication that depends heavily upon the speakers' shared context and is typically arrived at with the first two years of exposure to English. CALP is a more specialized application of English that depends on vocabulary and modality rather than shared context, and requires on average five or more years for a student to gain academic proficiency appropriate to his grade level.

69. A: lighten the student's cultural load. Cultural load refers to the ways in which language and culture interact and contribute to one another. By showing curiosity and interest toward an ELL's L1, the teacher is helping to lighten her cultural load.

70. A: A phoneme is the smallest unit of distinctive sound; a morpheme is the smallest unit of distinctive meaning. Sounds that make a phonemic difference in one language, such as /b/ and /v/ in English, may not be heard as distinctive in another language.

71. B: affective filter. The affective filter is created by negative emotions such as embarrassment, anxiety or insecurity that inhibit a speaker's willingness to take risks necessary for language learning. The higher the affective filter, the less likely the student will be to take risks.

72. A: Qualified teachers must offer the bilingual instruction. The Civil Rights Language Minority Regulations of 1980 set policy for the identification, assessment, services offered and exit strategies for bilingual students, and required that teachers must be trained and qualified.

73. D: four to seven years. By the time an L2 learner graduates from high school and after four to seven years of instruction at a high level of quality, she will be as successful as L1s.

74. C: two-way immersion. Two-way immersion teaches L1 and L2 students equally with content instruction in both languages. L2 learners gain fluency with English as well as the content areas, while L1 learners gain fluency with a second language as well as the content areas. Biliteracy, academic achievement and appreciation of both cultures are the goals.

75. D: K–6, 40%. Late-exit bilingual programs are designed for students through 6th grade, offering L2 instruction at least 40% of the time.

76. C: tier 3 words. Tier 1 words are basic, high frequency and regular in spelling. Beyond initial instruction, none is needed. Tier 2 words are also high-frequency but spelling is irregular, and students who lack a rich vocabulary may not recognize them. Specific instruction is required. Tier 3 words are those used in limited, specific

contexts, such as an area of study. They should be taught prior to a lesson so that text or oral information will be understood.

77. D: *a* and *c*. Classifying students, exiting English proficient students, selecting assessment choices prior to annual state criterion referenced tests and determining the appropriate assessment option for LEP students before the administration of the state criterion referenced test each year are all possible tasks for Language Proficiency Assessment committees.

78. D: all the above. Opponents of bilingual programs fear: that students with an original language other than English will view being taught in their L1 as an easier way; that such students and adults will be less likely to integrate into the community and more likely to form culturally closed units; that such programs are costly to implement and that American-born students will suffer as a result. In reality, these arguments have been largely disproved by research.

79. A: final examinations, state and national tests, college-entrance exams. Summative assessments are those that are applied when instruction is complete in order to analyze results and improve future instruction.

80. D: 20. The Bilingual Education and Training Act of 1973 mandated that public schools with 20 or more LEP students per grade level must provide bilingual instruction. Permitting instruction in students' language was a death-blow to the practice of punishing students for using Spanish, called the "no Spanish rule."

81. A: in the mid-70s, when South Vietnam, Laos and Cambodian governments were in crisis and hundreds of thousands of refugees fled.

82. D: true. According to the study, no programs reported that more than 50% of English language-majority speakers were eligible for free lunch, or that less than 50% of language-minority speakers received free lunch. This suggests the economic level of L2 learners is lower-income.

83. C: the idea that new knowledge should be offered at a level just slightly above the learner's current knowledge. Krashen's model is based on the theory that information that is too complex is not readily absorbed.

84. B: be given instruction they are capable of understanding. With Lau vs. Nichols, the Supreme Court ruled that refusing to allow a student to participate in a program because of her degree of fluency is illegal.

85. D: assimilation; acculturation. When a member of one culture is absorbed into a more dominant culture, it is assimilation. As a result of assimilation, cultural identity, belief systems, language and other social and cultural markers are abandoned. With acculturation, a member of a minority culture is simultaneously influenced by the dominant culture and influences it.

86. A: Students will learn to identify types of mammal homes by name (burrow, nest, den, lair, lodge, etc.). Students will be able to discuss where these homes can be found. Students will be able to speculate about how these homes are constructed through drawing, writing, charting or graphically organizing their ideas. Answer (b) is far too specific to be useful, answer (c) is far too vague and answer (d) is too sophisticated a set of expectations given the age of the students. The goal of writing outcomes for any particular lesson is that the teacher clarifies for herself and for her students her goals in teaching the lessons. Verbs such as *research, explain, listen, discuss, write, read* and *list* help the teacher focus on her goals, and give students explicit instructions.

87. D: rubrics. A rubrics is a type of formative assessment often used for self-assessment to monitor ongoing results.

88. D: all the above. Enlightened Eclecticism, Total Physical Response, Humanistic Approach, Silent Way, Natural Approach, and Suggestopedia are all variations of a communicative approach in which the teacher's role is that of a catalyst.

89. B: These sounds are not distinct in their L1 phonemes, and so are 'invisible.' When students with a language of origin other than English encounter a phoneme that is distinct in English but not in their language(s), the student does not 'hear' a distinction. The words 'raw' and 'law' sound alike to many Japanese students, while 'berry' and 'very' may be difficult for Spanish learners to hear.

90. A: stages of language development. Language acquisition begins with a silent period in which there is some minimal understanding of word meanings, but no meaningful orality. Next, at the early production level, comprehension increases somewhat, and verbal expressions are limited to one or two words or sounds. Following this is the speech emergence stage, where simple sentences with underlying errors in pronunciation and grammar are inevitable. Comprehension and speaking ability has greatly improved by the intermediate fluency stage.

91. B: parents. A site committee is made up of teachers, Para pros and other school employees, as well as an LEP's parent(s) and, if appropriate, the student himself.

92. D: communication between parents and school administrators in a language parents can understand. Title VII requires that districts with more than 5% of the student population from other countries provide second language instruction for those students. This act also forbids placing LEP students in handicapped or vocational classes based on lack of language proficiency only.

93. B: reciprocal teaching. Summarizing, question generating, clarifying, and predicting are combined strategies used with a reciprocal teaching approach. Reciprocal teaching advocates classroom dialogue with the goal of a deeper understanding of the meanings in a particular text. Summarizing integrates the

broadest and most important pieces of information in the text by locating them across sentences, paragraphs, or the text as a whole. Question generating is the next step toward reading comprehension. In order to generate authentic questions, readers must recognize significant information. The act of clarifying causes students to concentrate not just on what a passage says, but on progressively deeper levels of complexity, especially considering the reasons a particular passage might seem obscure (concepts that are complex and new, unfamiliar vocabulary, unexpected arguments, etc.). Predicting is the act of theorizing the text's next point or argument, and involves students' prior knowledge, a sense of the author's writing style, point of view and purpose, and an understanding of the organizing principals of the text such as chapter headings, subheadings and parenthetical asides.

94. C: 5 years or more. Cognitive Academic Language Proficiency (CALP) takes considerably longer to develop than Basic Interpersonal Communication Skills (BICS)—usually about 5–7 years. CALP skills are important to literacy and academic success.

95. A: work that requires students to recall academic language and generate written or spoken discourse that depends upon it. When students must consult memory to retrieve a specific word or use language specific to a particular area in written discourse, he is performing content-based tasks.

96. A: the Bilingual Syntax Measure (BSM). Both BSM and BINL are designed to assess oral language skills. BINL uses story re-telling involving a visual image, while BSM relies upon questions that require short answers in response.

97. C: SUP. According to the Separate Underlying Proficiency theory, there is no relationship between L1 and L2 language acquisition.

98. A: syllabic; logographic. Syllabic writing systems serve languages with a limited number of syllable constructions, because each is represented by one symbol. Japanese has about a hundred syllables. Logographic systems of writing are sometimes called pictographic or ideographic, because the written form offers simplified pictures of objects, activities and ideas they represent.

99. D: using language as a medium for the message, rather than making the memorizing of its rules an end in itself. Task-based strategies involve the learner in a variety of efforts that involve and are served by language but do not focus on the learning of rules or vocabulary as an end in itself.

100. B: Learning; knowing about; acquisition; unconscious. In Language Acquisition Theory, learning, or knowing about a language is conscious and directed, while acquiring or taking ownership of a language is unconscious.

Secret Key #1 - Time is Your Greatest Enemy

Pace Yourself

Wear a watch. At the beginning of the test, check the time (or start a chronometer on your watch to count the minutes), and check the time after every few questions to make sure you are "on schedule."

If you are forced to speed up, do it efficiently. Usually one or more answer choices can be eliminated without too much difficulty. Above all, don't panic. Don't speed up and just begin guessing at random choices. By pacing yourself, and continually monitoring your progress against your watch, you will always know exactly how far ahead or behind you are with your available time. If you find that you are one minute behind on the test, don't skip one question without spending any time on it, just to catch back up. Take 15 fewer seconds on the next four questions, and after four questions you'll have caught back up. Once you catch back up, you can continue working each problem at your normal pace.

Furthermore, don't dwell on the problems that you were rushed on. If a problem was taking up too much time and you made a hurried guess, it must be difficult. The difficult questions are the ones you are most likely to miss anyway, so it isn't a big loss. It is better to end with more time than you need than to run out of time.

Lastly, sometimes it is beneficial to slow down if you are constantly getting ahead of time. You are always more likely to catch a careless mistake by working more slowly than quickly, and among very high-scoring test takers (those who are likely to have lots of time left over), careless errors affect the score more than mastery of material.

Secret Key #2 - Guessing is not Guesswork

You probably know that guessing is a good idea. Unlike other standardized tests, there is no penalty for getting a wrong answer. Even if you have no idea about a question, you still have a 20-25% chance of getting it right.

Most test takers do not understand the impact that proper guessing can have on their score. Unless you score extremely high, guessing will significantly contribute to your final score.

Monkeys Take the Test

What most test takers don't realize is that to insure that 20-25% chance, you have to guess randomly. If you put 20 monkeys in a room to take this test, assuming they answered once per question and behaved themselves, on average they would get 20-25% of the questions correct. Put 20 test takers in the room, and the average will be much lower among guessed questions. Why?

1. The test writers intentionally write deceptive answer choices that "look" right. A test taker has no idea about a question, so he picks the "best looking" answer, which is often wrong. The monkey has no idea what looks good and what doesn't, so it will consistently be right about 20-25% of the time.
2. Test takers will eliminate answer choices from the guessing pool based on a hunch or intuition. Simple but correct answers often get excluded, leaving a 0% chance of being correct. The monkey has no clue, and often gets lucky with the best choice.

This is why the process of elimination endorsed by most test courses is flawed and detrimental to your performance. Test takers don't guess; they make an ignorant stab in the dark that is usually worse than random.

$5 Challenge

Let me introduce one of the most valuable ideas of this course—the $5 challenge:

You only mark your "best guess" if you are willing to bet $5 on it.
You only eliminate choices from guessing if you are willing to bet $5 on it.

Why $5? Five dollars is an amount of money that is small yet not insignificant, and can really add up fast (20 questions could cost you $100). Likewise, each answer choice on one question of the test will have a small impact on your overall score, but it can really add up to a lot of points in the end.

The process of elimination IS valuable. The following shows your chance of guessing it right:

If you eliminate wrong answer choices until only this many remain:	Chance of getting it correct:
1	100%
2	50%
3	33%

However, if you accidentally eliminate the right answer or go on a hunch for an incorrect answer, your chances drop dramatically—to 0%. By guessing among all the answer choices, you are GUARANTEED to have a shot at the right answer.

That's why the $5 test is so valuable. If you give up the advantage and safety of a pure guess, it had better be worth the risk.

What we still haven't covered is how to be sure that whatever guess you make is truly random. Here's the easiest way:

Always pick the first answer choice among those remaining.

Such a technique means that you have decided, **before you see a single test question**, exactly how you are going to guess, and since the order of choices tells you nothing about which one is correct, this guessing technique is perfectly random. This section is not meant to scare you away from making educated guesses or eliminating choices; you just need to define when a choice is worth eliminating. The $5 test, along with a pre-defined random guessing strategy, is the best way to make sure you reap all of the benefits of guessing.

Secret Key #3 - Practice Smarter, Not Harder

Many test takers delay the test preparation process because they dread the awful amounts of practice time they think necessary to succeed on the test. We have refined an effective method that will take you only a fraction of the time.

There are a number of "obstacles" in the path to success. Among these are answering questions, finishing in time, and mastering test-taking strategies. All must be executed on the day of the test at peak performance, or your score will suffer. The test is a mental marathon that has a large impact on your future.

Just like a marathon runner, it is important to work your way up to the full challenge. So first you just worry about questions, and then time, and finally strategy:

Success Strategy

1. Find a good source for practice tests.
2. If you are willing to make a larger time investment, consider using more than one study guide. Often the different approaches of multiple authors will help you "get" difficult concepts.
3. Take a practice test with no time constraints, with all study helps, "open book." Take your time with questions and focus on applying strategies.
4. Take a practice test with time constraints, with all guides, "open book."
5. Take a final practice test without open material and with time limits.

If you have time to take more practice tests, just repeat step 5. By gradually exposing yourself to the full rigors of the test environment, you will condition your mind to the stress of test day and maximize your success.

Secret Key #4 - Prepare, Don't Procrastinate

Let me state an obvious fact: if you take the test three times, you will probably get three different scores. This is due to the way you feel on test day, the level of preparedness you have, and the version of the test you see. Despite the test writers' claims to the contrary, some versions of the test WILL be easier for you than others.

Since your future depends so much on your score, you should maximize your chances of success. In order to maximize the likelihood of success, you've got to prepare in advance. This means taking practice tests and spending time learning the information and test taking strategies you will need to succeed.

Never go take the actual test as a "practice" test, expecting that you can just take it again if you need to. Take all the practice tests you can on your own, but when you go to take the official test, be prepared, be focused, and do your best the first time!

Secret Key #5 - Test Yourself

Everyone knows that time is money. There is no need to spend too much of your time or too little of your time preparing for the test. You should only spend as much of your precious time preparing as is necessary for you to get the score you need.

Once you have taken a practice test under real conditions of time constraints, then you will know if you are ready for the test or not.

If you have scored extremely high the first time that you take the practice test, then there is not much point in spending countless hours studying. You are already there.

Benchmark your abilities by retaking practice tests and seeing how much you have improved. Once you consistently score high enough to guarantee success, then you are ready.

If you have scored well below where you need, then knuckle down and begin studying in earnest. Check your improvement regularly through the use of practice tests under real conditions. Above all, don't worry, panic, or give up. The key is perseverance!

Then, when you go to take the test, remain confident and remember how well you did on the practice tests. If you can score high enough on a practice test, then you can do the same on the real thing.

General Strategies

The most important thing you can do is to ignore your fears and jump into the test immediately. Do not be overwhelmed by any strange-sounding terms. You have to jump into the test like jumping into a pool—all at once is the easiest way.

Make Predictions

As you read and understand the question, try to guess what the answer will be. Remember that several of the answer choices are wrong, and once you begin reading them, your mind will immediately become cluttered with answer choices designed to throw you off. Your mind is typically the most focused immediately after you have read the question and digested its contents. If you can, try to predict what the correct answer will be. You may be surprised at what you can predict.

Quickly scan the choices and see if your prediction is in the listed answer choices. If it is, then you can be quite confident that you have the right answer. It still won't hurt to check the other answer choices, but most of the time, you've got it!

Answer the Question

It may seem obvious to only pick answer choices that answer the question, but the test writers can create some excellent answer choices that are wrong. Don't pick an answer just because it sounds right, or you believe it to be true. It MUST answer the question. Once you've made your selection, always go back and check it against the question and make sure that you didn't misread the question and that the answer choice does answer the question posed.

Benchmark

After you read the first answer choice, decide if you think it sounds correct or not. If it doesn't, move on to the next answer choice. If it does, mentally mark that answer choice. This doesn't mean that you've definitely selected it as your answer choice, it just means that it's the best you've seen thus far. Go ahead and read the next choice. If the next choice is worse than the one you've already selected, keep going to the next answer choice. If the next choice is better than the choice you've already selected, mentally mark the new answer choice as your best guess.

The first answer choice that you select becomes your standard. Every other answer choice must be benchmarked against that standard. That choice is correct until proven otherwise by another answer choice beating it out. Once you've decided that no other answer choice seems as good, do one final check to ensure that your answer choice answers the question posed.

Valid Information

Don't discount any of the information provided in the question. Every piece of information may be necessary to determine the correct answer. None of the information in the question is there to throw you off (while the answer choices will certainly have information to throw you off). If two seemingly unrelated topics are discussed, don't ignore either. You can be confident there is a relationship, or it wouldn't be included in the question, and you are probably going to have to determine what is that relationship to find the answer.

Avoid "Fact Traps"

Don't get distracted by a choice that is factually true. Your search is for the answer that answers the question. Stay focused and don't fall for an answer that is true but irrelevant. Always go back to the question and make sure you're choosing an answer that actually answers the question and is not just a true statement. An answer can be factually correct, but it MUST answer the question asked. Additionally, two answers can both be seemingly correct, so be sure to read all of the answer choices, and make sure that you get the one that BEST answers the question.

Milk the Question

Some of the questions may throw you completely off. They might deal with a subject you have not been exposed to, or one that you haven't reviewed in years. While your lack of knowledge about the subject will be a hindrance, the question itself can give you many clues that will help you find the correct answer. Read the question carefully and look for clues. Watch particularly for adjectives and nouns describing difficult terms or words that you don't recognize. Regardless of whether you completely understand a word or not, replacing it with a synonym, either provided or one you more familiar with, may help you to understand what the questions are asking. Rather than wracking your mind about specific detailed information concerning a difficult term or word, try to use mental substitutes that are easier to understand.

The Trap of Familiarity

Don't just choose a word because you recognize it. On difficult questions, you may not recognize a number of words in the answer choices. The test writers don't put "make-believe" words on the test, so don't think that just because you only recognize all the words in one answer choice that that answer choice must be correct. If you only recognize words in one answer choice, then focus on that one. Is it correct? Try your best to determine if it is correct. If it is, that's great. If not, eliminate it. Each word and answer choice you eliminate increases your chances of getting the question correct, even if you then have to guess among the unfamiliar choices.

Eliminate Answers

Eliminate choices as soon as you realize they are wrong. But be careful! Make sure you consider all of the possible answer choices. Just because one appears right, doesn't mean that the next one won't be even better! The test writers will usually put more than one good answer choice for every question, so read all of them. Don't worry if you are stuck between two that seem right. By getting down to just two remaining possible choices, your odds are now 50/50. Rather than wasting too much time, play the odds. You are guessing, but guessing wisely because you've been able to knock out some of the answer choices that you know are wrong. If you are eliminating choices and realize that the last answer choice you are left with is also obviously wrong, don't panic. Start over and consider each choice again. There may easily be something that you missed the first time and will realize on the second pass.

Tough Questions

If you are stumped on a problem or it appears too hard or too difficult, don't waste time. Move on! Remember though, if you can quickly check for obviously incorrect answer choices, your chances of guessing correctly are greatly improved. Before you completely give up, at least try to knock out a couple of possible answers. Eliminate what you can and then guess at the remaining answer choices before moving on.

Brainstorm

If you get stuck on a difficult question, spend a few seconds quickly brainstorming. Run through the complete list of possible answer choices. Look at each choice and ask yourself, "Could this answer the question satisfactorily?" Go through each answer choice and consider it independently of the others. By systematically going through all possibilities, you may find something that you would otherwise overlook. Remember though that when you get stuck, it's important to try to keep moving.

Read Carefully

Understand the problem. Read the question and answer choices carefully. Don't miss the question because you misread the terms. You have plenty of time to read each question thoroughly and make sure you understand what is being asked. Yet a happy medium must be attained, so don't waste too much time. You must read carefully, but efficiently.

Face Value

When in doubt, use common sense. Always accept the situation in the problem at face value. Don't read too much into it. These problems will not require you to make huge leaps of logic. The test writers aren't trying to throw you off with a cheap trick. If you have to go beyond creativity and make a leap of logic in order to have an answer choice answer the question, then you should look at the other answer choices. Don't overcomplicate the problem by creating theoretical relationships or explanations that will warp time or space. These are normal problems rooted in reality. It's just that the applicable relationship or explanation may not be readily apparent and you have to figure things out. Use your common sense to interpret anything that isn't clear.

Prefixes

If you're having trouble with a word in the question or answer choices, try dissecting it. Take advantage of every clue that the word might include. Prefixes and suffixes can be a huge help. Usually they allow you to determine a basic meaning. Pre- means before, post- means after, pro - is positive, de- is negative. From these prefixes and suffixes, you can get an idea of the general meaning of the word and try to put it into context. Beware though of any traps. Just because con- is the opposite of pro-, doesn't necessarily mean congress is the opposite of progress!

Hedge Phrases

Watch out for critical hedge phrases, led off with words such as "likely," "may," "can," "sometimes," "often," "almost," "mostly," "usually," "generally," "rarely," and "sometimes." Question writers insert these hedge phrases to cover every possibility. Often an answer choice will be wrong simply because it leaves no room for exception. Unless the situation calls for them, avoid answer choices that have definitive words like "exactly," and "always."

Switchback Words

Stay alert for "switchbacks." These are the words and phrases frequently used to alert you to shifts in thought. The most common switchback word is "but." Others include "although," "however," "nevertheless," "on the other hand," "even though," "while," "in spite of," "despite," and "regardless of."

New Information

Correct answer choices will rarely have completely new information included. Answer choices typically are straightforward reflections of the material asked about and will directly relate to the question. If a new piece of information is included in an answer choice that doesn't even seem to relate to the topic being asked about, then that answer choice is likely incorrect. All of the information needed to answer the question is usually provided for you in the question. You should not have to make guesses that are unsupported or choose answer choices that require unknown information that cannot be reasoned from what is given.

Time Management

On technical questions, don't get lost on the technical terms. Don't spend too much time on any one question. If you don't know what a term means, then odds are you aren't going to get much further since you don't have a dictionary. You should be able to immediately recognize whether or not you know a term. If you don't, work with the other clues that you have—the other answer choices and terms provided— but don't waste too much time trying to figure out a difficult term that you don't know.

Contextual Clues

Look for contextual clues. An answer can be right but not the correct answer. The contextual clues will help you find the answer that is most right and is correct. Understand the context in which a phrase or statement is made. This will help you make important distinctions.

Don't Panic

Panicking will not answer any questions for you; therefore, it isn't helpful. When you first see the question, if your mind goes blank, take a deep breath. Force yourself to mechanically go through the steps of solving the problem using the strategies you've learned.

Pace Yourself

Don't get clock fever. It's easy to be overwhelmed when you're looking at a page full of questions, your mind is full of random thoughts and feeling confused, and the clock is ticking down faster than you would like. Calm down and maintain the pace that you have set for yourself. As long as you are on track by monitoring your pace, you are guaranteed to have enough time for yourself. When you get to the last few minutes of the test, it may seem like you won't have enough time left, but if you only have as many questions as you should have left at that point, then you're right on track!

Answer Selection

The best way to pick an answer choice is to eliminate all of those that are wrong, until only one is left and confirm that is the correct answer. Sometimes though, an answer choice may immediately look right. Be careful! Take a second to make sure that the other choices are not equally obvious. Don't make a hasty mistake. There are only two times that you should stop before checking other answers. First is when you are positive that the answer choice you have selected is correct. Second is when time is almost out and you have to make a quick guess!

Check Your Work

Since you will probably not know every term listed and the answer to every question, it is important that you get credit for the ones that you do know. Don't miss any questions through careless mistakes. If at all possible, try to take a second to look back over your answer selection and make sure you've selected the correct answer choice and haven't made a costly careless mistake (such as marking an answer choice that you didn't mean to mark). The time it takes for this quick double check should more than pay for itself in caught mistakes.

Beware of Directly Quoted Answers

Sometimes an answer choice will repeat word for word a portion of the question or reference section. However, beware of such exact duplication. It may be a trap! More than likely, the correct choice will paraphrase or summarize a point, rather than being exactly the same wording.

Slang

Scientific sounding answers are better than slang ones. An answer choice that begins "To compare the outcomes..." is much more likely to be correct than one that begins "Because some people insisted..."

Extreme Statements

Avoid wild answers that throw out highly controversial ideas that are proclaimed as established fact. An answer choice that states the "process should used in certain situations, if..." is much more likely to be correct than one that states the "process should be discontinued completely." The first is a calm rational statement and doesn't even make a definitive, uncompromising stance, using a hedge word "if" to provide wiggle room, whereas the second choice is a radical idea and far more extreme.

Answer Choice Families

When you have two or more answer choices that are direct opposites or parallels, one of them is usually the correct answer. For instance, if one answer choice states "x increases" and another answer choice states "x decreases" or "y increases," then those two or three answer choices are very similar in construction and fall into the same family of answer choices. A family of answer choices consists of two or three answer choices, very similar in construction, but often with directly opposite meanings. Usually the correct answer choice will be in that family of answer choices. The "odd man out" or answer choice that doesn't seem to fit the parallel construction of the other answer choices is more likely to be incorrect.

Special Report: How to Overcome Test Anxiety

The very nature of tests caters to some level of anxiety, nervousness, or tension, just as we feel for any important event that occurs in our lives. A little bit of anxiety or nervousness can be a good thing. It helps us with motivation, and makes achievement just that much sweeter. However, too much anxiety can be a problem, especially if it hinders our ability to function and perform.

"Test anxiety," is the term that refers to the emotional reactions that some test-takers experience when faced with a test or exam. Having a fear of testing and exams is based upon a rational fear, since the test-taker's performance can shape the course of an academic career. Nevertheless, experiencing excessive fear of examinations will only interfere with the test-taker's ability to perform and chance to be successful.

There are a large variety of causes that can contribute to the development and sensation of test anxiety. These include, but are not limited to, lack of preparation and worrying about issues surrounding the test.

Lack of Preparation

Lack of preparation can be identified by the following behaviors or situations:
- Not scheduling enough time to study, and therefore cramming the night before the test or exam
- Managing time poorly, to create the sensation that there is not enough time to do everything
- Failing to organize the text information in advance, so that the study material consists of the entire text and not simply the pertinent information
- Poor overall studying habits

Worrying, on the other hand, can be related to both the test taker, or many other factors around him/her that will be affected by the results of the test. These include worrying about:
- Previous performances on similar exams, or exams in general
- How friends and other students are achieving
- The negative consequences that will result from a poor grade or failure

There are three primary elements to test anxiety. Physical components, which involve the same typical bodily reactions as those to acute anxiety (to be discussed below). Emotional factors have to do with fear or panic. Mental or cognitive issues concerning attention spans and memory abilities.

Physical Signals

There are many different symptoms of test anxiety, and these are not limited to mental and emotional strain. Frequently there are a range of physical signals that will let a test taker know that he/she is suffering from test anxiety. These bodily changes can include the following:

- Perspiring
- Sweaty palms
- Wet, trembling hands
- Nausea
- Dry mouth
- A knot in the stomach
- Headache
- Faintness
- Muscle tension
- Aching shoulders, back and neck
- Rapid heart beat
- Feeling too hot/cold

To recognize the sensation of test anxiety, a test-taker should monitor him/herself for the following sensations:

- The physical distress symptoms as listed above
- Emotional sensitivity, expressing emotional feelings such as the need to cry or laugh too much, or a sensation of anger or helplessness
- A decreased ability to think, causing the test-taker to blank out or have racing thoughts that are hard to organize or control

Though most students will feel some level of anxiety when faced with a test or exam, the majority can cope with that anxiety and maintain it at a manageable level. However, those who cannot are faced with a very real and very serious condition, which can and should be controlled for the immeasurable benefit of this sufferer.

Naturally, these sensations lead to negative results for the testing experience. The most common effects of test anxiety have to do with nervousness and mental blocking.

Nervousness

Nervousness can appear in several different levels:

- The test-taker's difficulty, or even inability to read and understand the questions on the test
- The difficulty or inability to organize thoughts to a coherent form

- The difficulty or inability to recall key words and concepts relating to the testing questions (especially essays)
- The receipt of poor grades on a test, though the test material was well known by the test taker

Conversely, a person may also experience mental blocking, which involves:
- Blanking out on test questions
- Only remembering the correct answers to the questions when the test has already finished

Fortunately for test anxiety sufferers, beating these feelings, to a large degree, has to do with proper preparation. When a test taker has a feeling of preparedness, then anxiety will be dramatically lessened.

The first step to resolving anxiety issues is to distinguish which of the two types of anxiety are being suffered. If the anxiety is a direct result of a lack of preparation, this should be considered a normal reaction, and the anxiety level (as opposed to the test results) shouldn't be anything to worry about. However, if, when adequately prepared, the test-taker still panics, blanks out, or seems to overreact, this is not a fully rational reaction. While this can be considered normal too, there are many ways to combat and overcome these effects.

Remember that anxiety cannot be entirely eliminated, however, there are ways to minimize it, to make the anxiety easier to manage. Preparation is one of the best ways to minimize test anxiety. Therefore the following techniques are wise in order to best fight off any anxiety that may want to build.

To begin with, try to avoid cramming before a test, whenever it is possible. By trying to memorize an entire term's worth of information in one day, you'll be shocking your system, and not giving yourself a very good chance to absorb the information. This is an easy path to anxiety, so for those who suffer from test anxiety, cramming should not even be considered an option.

Instead of cramming, work throughout the semester to combine all of the material which is presented throughout the semester, and work on it gradually as the course goes by, making sure to master the main concepts first, leaving minor details for a week or so before the test.

To study for the upcoming exam, be sure to pose questions that may be on the examination, to gauge the ability to answer them by integrating the ideas from your texts, notes and lectures, as well as any supplementary readings.

If it is truly impossible to cover all of the information that was covered in that particular term, concentrate on the most important portions, that can be covered very well. Learn these concepts as best as possible, so that when the test comes, a goal can be made to use these concepts as presentations of your knowledge.

In addition to study habits, changes in attitude are critical to beating a struggle with test anxiety. In fact, an improvement of the perspective over the entire test-taking experience can actually help a test taker to enjoy studying and therefore improve the overall experience. Be certain not to overemphasize the significance of the grade - know that the result of the test is neither a reflection of self worth, nor is it a measure of intelligence; one grade will not predict a person's future success.

To improve an overall testing outlook, the following steps should be tried:
- Keeping in mind that the most reasonable expectation for taking a test is to expect to try to demonstrate as much of what you know as you possibly can.
- Reminding ourselves that a test is only one test; this is not the only one, and there will be others.
- The thought of thinking of oneself in an irrational, all-or-nothing term should be avoided at all costs.
- A reward should be designated for after the test, so there's something to look forward to. Whether it be going to a movie, going out to eat, or simply visiting friends, schedule it in advance, and do it no matter what result is expected on the exam.

Test-takers should also keep in mind that the basics are some of the most important things, even beyond anti-anxiety techniques and studying. Never neglect the basic social, emotional and biological needs, in order to try to absorb information. In order to best achieve, these three factors must be held as just as important as the studying itself.

Study Steps

Remember the following important steps for studying:
- Maintain healthy nutrition and exercise habits. Continue both your recreational activities and social pass times. These both contribute to your physical and emotional well being.
- Be certain to get a good amount of sleep, especially the night before the test, because when you're overtired you are not able to perform to the best of your best ability.
- Keep the studying pace to a moderate level by taking breaks when they are needed, and varying the work whenever possible, to keep the mind fresh instead of getting bored.
- When enough studying has been done that all the material that can be learned has been learned, and the test taker is prepared for the test, stop

studying and do something relaxing such as listening to music, watching a movie, or taking a warm bubble bath.

There are also many other techniques to minimize the uneasiness or apprehension that is experienced along with test anxiety before, during, or even after the examination. In fact, there are a great deal of things that can be done to stop anxiety from interfering with lifestyle and performance. Again, remember that anxiety will not be eliminated entirely, and it shouldn't be. Otherwise that "up" feeling for exams would not exist, and most of us depend on that sensation to perform better than usual. However, this anxiety has to be at a level that is manageable.

Of course, as we have just discussed, being prepared for the exam is half the battle right away. Attending all classes, finding out what knowledge will be expected on the exam, and knowing the exam schedules are easy steps to lowering anxiety. Keeping up with work will remove the need to cram, and efficient study habits will eliminate wasted time. Studying should be done in an ideal location for concentration, so that it is simple to become interested in the material and give it complete attention. A method such as SQ3R (Survey, Question, Read, Recite, Review) is a wonderful key to follow to make sure that the study habits are as effective as possible, especially in the case of learning from a textbook. Flashcards are great techniques for memorization. Learning to take good notes will mean that notes will be full of useful information, so that less sifting will need to be done to seek out what is pertinent for studying. Reviewing notes after class and then again on occasion will keep the information fresh in the mind. From notes that have been taken summary sheets and outlines can be made for simpler reviewing.

A study group can also be a very motivational and helpful place to study, as there will be a sharing of ideas, all of the minds can work together, to make sure that everyone understands, and the studying will be made more interesting because it will be a social occasion.

Basically, though, as long as the test-taker remains organized and self confident, with efficient study habits, less time will need to be spent studying, and higher grades will be achieved.

To become self confident, there are many useful steps. The first of these is "self talk." It has been shown through extensive research, that self-talk for students who suffer from test anxiety, should be well monitored, in order to make sure that it contributes to self confidence as opposed to sinking the student. Frequently the self talk of test-anxious students is negative or self-defeating, thinking that everyone else is smarter and faster, that they always mess up, and that if they don't do well, they'll fail the entire course. It is important to decreasing anxiety that awareness is made of self talk. Try writing any negative self thoughts and then disputing them with a positive statement instead. Begin self-encouragement as though it was a friend speaking. Repeat positive statements to help reprogram the mind to believing in successes instead of failures.

Helpful Techniques

Other extremely helpful techniques include:
- Self-visualization of doing well and reaching goals
- While aiming for an "A" level of understanding, don't try to "overprotect" by setting your expectations lower. This will only convince the mind to stop studying in order to meet the lower expectations.
- Don't make comparisons with the results or habits of other students. These are individual factors, and different things work for different people, causing different results.
- Strive to become an expert in learning what works well, and what can be done in order to improve. Consider collecting this data in a journal.
- Create rewards for after studying instead of doing things before studying that will only turn into avoidance behaviors.
- Make a practice of relaxing - by using methods such as progressive relaxation, self-hypnosis, guided imagery, etc - in order to make relaxation an automatic sensation.
- Work on creating a state of relaxed concentration so that concentrating will take on the focus of the mind, so that none will be wasted on worrying.
- Take good care of the physical self by eating well and getting enough sleep.
- Plan in time for exercise and stick to this plan.

Beyond these techniques, there are other methods to be used before, during and after the test that will help the test-taker perform well in addition to overcoming anxiety.

Before the exam comes the academic preparation. This involves establishing a study schedule and beginning at least one week before the actual date of the test. By doing this, the anxiety of not having enough time to study for the test will be automatically eliminated. Moreover, this will make the studying a much more effective experience, ensuring that the learning will be an easier process. This relieves much undue pressure on the test-taker.

Summary sheets, note cards, and flash cards with the main concepts and examples of these main concepts should be prepared in advance of the actual studying time. A topic should never be eliminated from this process. By omitting a topic because it isn't expected to be on the test is only setting up the test-taker for anxiety should it actually appear on the exam. Utilize the course syllabus for laying out the topics that should be studied. Carefully go over the notes that were made in class, paying special attention to any of the issues that the professor took special care to emphasize while lecturing in class. In the textbooks, use the chapter review, or if possible, the chapter tests, to begin your review.

It may even be possible to ask the instructor what information will be covered on the exam, or what the format of the exam will be (for example, multiple choice, essay, free form, true-false). Additionally, see if it is possible to find out how many questions will be on the test. If a review sheet or sample test has been offered by the professor, make good use of it, above anything else, for the preparation for the test. Another great resource for getting to know the examination is reviewing tests from previous semesters. Use these tests to review, and aim to achieve a 100% score on each of the possible topics. With a few exceptions, the goal that you set for yourself is the highest one that you will reach.

Take all of the questions that were assigned as homework, and rework them to any other possible course material. The more problems reworked, the more skill and confidence will form as a result. When forming the solution to a problem, write out each of the steps. Don't simply do head work. By doing as many steps on paper as possible, much clarification and therefore confidence will be formed. Do this with as many homework problems as possible, before checking the answers. By checking the answer after each problem, a reinforcement will exist, that will not be on the exam. Study situations should be as exam-like as possible, to prime the test-taker's system for the experience. By waiting to check the answers at the end, a psychological advantage will be formed, to decrease the stress factor.

Another fantastic reason for not cramming is the avoidance of confusion in concepts, especially when it comes to mathematics. 8-10 hours of study will become one hundred percent more effective if it is spread out over a week or at least several days, instead of doing it all in one sitting. Recognize that the human brain requires time in order to assimilate new material, so frequent breaks and a span of study time over several days will be much more beneficial.

Additionally, don't study right up until the point of the exam. Studying should stop a minimum of one hour before the exam begins. This allows the brain to rest and put things in their proper order. This will also provide the time to become as relaxed as possible when going into the examination room. The test-taker will also have time to eat well and eat sensibly. Know that the brain needs food as much as the rest of the body. With enough food and enough sleep, as well as a relaxed attitude, the body and the mind are primed for success.

Avoid any anxious classmates who are talking about the exam. These students only spread anxiety, and are not worth sharing the anxious sentimentalities.

Before the test also involves creating a positive attitude, so mental preparation should also be a point of concentration. There are many keys to creating a positive attitude. Should fears become rushing in, make a visualization of taking the exam, doing well, and seeing an A written on the paper. Write out a list of affirmations that will bring a feeling of confidence, such as "I am doing well in my English class," "I studied well and know my material," "I enjoy this class." Even if the affirmations aren't believed at first, it sends a positive message to the subconscious which will result in an alteration of the overall belief system, which is the system that creates reality.

If a sensation of panic begins, work with the fear and imagine the very worst! Work through the entire scenario of not passing the test, failing the entire course, and dropping out of school, followed by not getting a job, and pushing a shopping cart through the dark alley where you'll live. This will place things into perspective! Then, practice deep breathing and create a visualization of the opposite situation - achieving an "A" on the exam, passing the entire course, receiving the degree at a graduation ceremony.

On the day of the test, there are many things to be done to ensure the best results, as well as the most calm outlook. The following stages are suggested in order to maximize test-taking potential:
- Begin the examination day with a moderate breakfast, and avoid any coffee or beverages with caffeine if the test taker is prone to jitters. Even people who are used to managing caffeine can feel jittery or light-headed when it is taken on a test day.
- Attempt to do something that is relaxing before the examination begins. As last minute cramming clouds the mastering of overall concepts, it is better to use this time to create a calming outlook.
- Be certain to arrive at the test location well in advance, in order to provide time to select a location that is away from doors, windows and other distractions, as well as giving enough time to relax before the test begins.
- Keep away from anxiety generating classmates who will upset the sensation of stability and relaxation that is being attempted before the exam.
- Should the waiting period before the exam begins cause anxiety, create a self-distraction by reading a light magazine or something else that is relaxing and simple.

During the exam itself, read the entire exam from beginning to end, and find out how much time should be allotted to each individual problem. Once writing the exam, should more time be taken for a problem, it should be abandoned, in order to begin another problem. If there is time at the end, the unfinished problem can always be returned to and completed.

Read the instructions very carefully - twice - so that unpleasant surprises won't follow during or after the exam has ended.

When writing the exam, pretend that the situation is actually simply the completion of homework within a library, or at home. This will assist in forming a relaxed atmosphere, and will allow the brain extra focus for the complex thinking function.

Begin the exam with all of the questions with which the most confidence is felt. This will build the confidence level regarding the entire exam and will begin a quality momentum. This will also create encouragement for trying the problems where uncertainty resides.

Going with the "gut instinct" is always the way to go when solving a problem. Second guessing should be avoided at all costs. Have confidence in the ability to do well.

For essay questions, create an outline in advance that will keep the mind organized and make certain that all of the points are remembered. For multiple choice, read every answer, even if the correct one has been spotted - a better one may exist.

Continue at a pace that is reasonable and not rushed, in order to be able to work carefully. Provide enough time to go over the answers at the end, to check for small errors that can be corrected.

Should a feeling of panic begin, breathe deeply, and think of the feeling of the body releasing sand through its pores. Visualize a calm, peaceful place, and include all of the sights, sounds and sensations of this image. Continue the deep breathing, and take a few minutes to continue this with closed eyes. When all is well again, return to the test.

If a "blanking" occurs for a certain question, skip it and move on to the next question. There will be time to return to the other question later. Get everything done that can be done, first, to guarantee all the grades that can be compiled, and to build all of the confidence possible. Then return to the weaker questions to build the marks from there.

Remember, one's own reality can be created, so as long as the belief is there, success will follow. And remember: anxiety can happen later, right now, there's an exam to be written!

After the examination is complete, whether there is a feeling for a good grade or a bad grade, don't dwell on the exam, and be certain to follow through on the reward that was promised...and enjoy it! Don't dwell on any mistakes that have been made, as there is nothing that can be done at this point anyway.

Additionally, don't begin to study for the next test right away. Do something relaxing for a while, and let the mind relax and prepare itself to begin absorbing information again.

From the results of the exam - both the grade and the entire experience, be certain to learn from what has gone on. Perfect studying habits and work some more on confidence in order to make the next examination experience even better than the last one.

Learn to avoid places where openings occurred for laziness, procrastination and day dreaming.

Use the time between this exam and the next one to better learn to relax, even learning to relax on cue, so that any anxiety can be controlled during the next exam. Learn how to relax the body. Slouch in your chair if that helps. Tighten and then relax all of the different muscle groups, one group at a time, beginning with the feet and then working all the way up to the neck and face. This will ultimately relax the muscles more than they were to begin with. Learn how to breathe deeply and comfortably, and focus on this breathing going in and out as a relaxing thought. With every exhale, repeat the word "relax."

As common as test anxiety is, it is very possible to overcome it. Make yourself one of the test-takers who overcome this frustrating hindrance.

Additional Bonus Material

Due to our efforts to try to keep this book to a manageable length, we've created a link that will give you access to all of your additional bonus material.

Please visit http://www.mometrix.com/bonus948/texesbiedsu to access the information.